ENDOMORPH DIET AND EXERCISE PLAN

Definitely Transform Your Body: The Essential Guide with Exercises to Boost Metabolism, Burn Fat and Weight Losse. Shape Your Body with a 30-Day Personalized Fast Food Plan for Any Age Without Sacrificing the Joy of Eating

MARK L. SHAW

© Copyright 2024 by Mark L. Shaw- All rights reserved.

This document is geared towards providing exact and reliable information in regard to the topic and issue covered.

- From a Declaration of Principles which was accepted and approved equally by a Committee of the American Bar Association and a Committee of Publishers and Associations.

In no way is it legal to reproduce, duplicate, or transmit any part of this document in either electronic means or in printed format. All rights reserved.

The information provided herein is stated to be truthful and consistent, in that any liability, in terms of inattention or otherwise, by any usage or abuse of any policies, processes, or directions contained within is the solitary and utter responsibility of the recipient reader. Under no circumstances will any legal responsibility or blame be held against the publisher for any reparation, damages, or monetary loss due to the information herein, either directly or indirectly.

Respective authors own all copyrights not held by the publisher.

The information herein is offered for informational purposes solely and is universal as so. The presentation of the information is without contract or any type of guarantee assurance.

The trademarks that are used are without any consent, and the publication of the trademark is without permission or backing by the trademark owner. All trademarks and brands within this book are for clarifying purposes only and are owned by the owners themselves, not affiliated with this document.

💥 HERE IS YOU FREE BONUS!
👇 SCAN HERE TO DOWNLOAD IT

1. All fitness levels welcome. Start at your level, push your boundaries.
2. Detailed guidance ensures injury-free, effective workouts.
3. Gym, home, full-body, the complete wellness package. Enhance your diet, boost wellness.

👇 SCAN HERE TO DOWNLOAD IT FOR FREE

TABLE OF CONTENTS

INTRODUCTION 6
Overview of somatotypes 7
The unique challenges and strengths of endomorphs 8
Strategies for Thriving as an Endomorph 8

PART I
UNDERSTANDING THE ENDOMORPHIC DIET 10

CHAPTER 1
FUNDAMENTALS OF ENDOMORPHIC NUTRITION 11
Understanding the Endomorphic Body Type 11
Nutritional Strategies for Endomorphs 12
Healthy Fats: Types and Benefits 14
Dietary Patterns and Meal Planning 14
Portion Control and Caloric Intake 15
Integrating Physical Activity with Nutritional Efforts 15
The importance of adaptability and being attentive to the body's cues 17
Effects of Macronutrient Manipulation on Metabolism 18
Fiber and Hydration: A Synergistic Relationship 19

CHAPTER 2
FOODS TO PREFER AND TO AVOID 21
Proteins for Satiety and Metabolic Boost 21
Fiber-Rich Vegetables and Fruits 22
Whole Grains and Low-Glycemic Carbohydrates 22
Healthy Fats for Hormonal Balance and Satiety 23
Herbs, Spices, and Condiments 24
Common nutritional pitfalls and the way to keep away from them 24
Choosing Processed Foods Over Whole Foods 25

PART II
BEYOND DIET AND EXERCISE 27

CHAPTER 3
HOLISTIC LIFESTYLE CHANGES FOR ENDOMORPHS 28
Diet and Nutrition for Endomorphs 28
Exercise and Physical Activity 30
Flexibility and Mobility Work 33

Stress Management and Sleep 34
The importance of constant and sustainable way of life changes 36

PART III
THE 30-DAY FOOD PLAN 38

CHAPTER 3
BASICS OF MEAL PLANNING 39
Macronutrient Ratios 39
Planning Meal 41
Setting your self up for success 42

CHAPTER 4
WEEK-THROUGH-WEEK GUIDE 44

PART IV
CUSTOMIZING THE EXERCISE REGIMEN 92

CHAPTER 5
TRAINING PRINCIPLES SPECIFIC TO ENDOMORPHS 93
High-Intensity Interval Training (HIIT) for Endomorphs 93
The Importance of Muscle Mass 94

PART V
MAINTAINING MOTIVATION AND OVERCOMING CHALLENGES 96

CHAPTER 6
MONITORING YOUR PROGRESS 97
The Importance of Setting Realistic Goals 97
Adapting the Plan to Evolving Needs 99
Implementing Technology and Tools 100

CHAPTER 7
SUCCESS STORIES 101
Sarah's Journey to Health and Happiness 101
John's Transformation from Couch Potato to Fitness Enthusiast 101
Emily's Journey to Self-Acceptance and Empowerment 102

BONUS CHAPTER
BUILDING YOUR TRAINING PLAN 103
Setting Your Goals 103
Selecting the Right Exercises 103
Designing Your Workout Schedule 103

CONCLUSION 106

INTRODUCTION

Understanding your frame kind is essential on the subject of fitness and nutrition. The endomorph frame kind, characterized by a bigger body and a better body fat percentage, frequently struggles with weight management. However, with a tailored food plan and exercising plan, individuals with an endomorph frame kind can effectively lose weight and improve their common fitness.

The endomorph body type is one of the 3 classifications within the somatotype concept, which additionally consists of ectomorphs and mesomorphs. Endomorphs are normally softer and rounder and generally tend to save fat effortlessly. Due to their bodily traits, endomorphs may discover it extra challenging to maintain a healthful weight. However, this does not mean that being an endomorph is a barrier to attaining health desires. It truly implies that their technique needs to be cautiously dependent and uniquely suitable to their physiological predispositions.

Diet plays a pivotal function in dealing with the endomorph body kind. Because endomorphs tend to have a slower metabolism, it's critical for them to recognition on a nutrition plan that reinforces metabolism and promotes fat burning. A low-carbohydrate, high-protein, and moderate-fats eating regimen can be specially powerful. This nutritional setup allows lessen the probability of fats storage by proscribing insulin spikes, which are greater dramatic in response to carbohydrate intake in endomorphs. Foods wealthy in fiber, together with vegetables and complete grains, ought to be prioritized as they assist maintain a sense of fullness and improve digestion.

Protein is mainly crucial for endomorphs. It allows in building lean muscles, that's beneficial as muscle burns extra calories at relaxation in comparison to fat. This can be a sizeable advantage in boosting the typically gradual metabolism of endomorphs. Good resources of lean protein include bird breast, turkey, fish, and plant-based proteins along with lentils and chickpeas. Fats should now not be absolutely discounted inside the food plan of an endomorph. However, the focal point ought to be on healthful fat which can aid in hormone regulation and provide electricity with out spiking insulin degrees. Avocados, nuts, seeds, and olive oil are outstanding assets of such fats.

In addition to weight loss plan, exercising is similarly vital. An effective workout plan for endomorphs need to include a mix of cardiovascular and electricity training activities. Cardiovascular physical games, together with going for walks, biking, or swimming, are essential for burning energy and enhancing coronary heart fitness. However, it is the electricity training that is regularly below-emphasised but vital for endomorphs. By growing muscle tissue, energy training enhances metabolic charge, supporting in burning more calories even at the same time as at relaxation.

High-intensity c programming language schooling (HIIT) can be specially useful for endomorphs. HIIT includes short bursts of extreme workout followed with the aid of rest or low-intensity durations. This sort of schooling is powerful in burning a excessive quantity of calories in a quick amount of time and may increase metabolic fee even after the exercise is completed. Consistency is fundamental in any food plan and exercise plan, but it's far especially crucial for endomorphs.

Due to their tendency to benefit weight without difficulty, normal tracking of diet and consistent exercise are important. Additionally, life-style factors inclusive of sleep and pressure control can not be unnoticed. Poor sleep and excessive pressure stages can lead to hormonal imbalances that make weight management even extra tough. Setting practical desires and know-how that development may be slower than for different frame kinds can help preserve motivation. It's crucial for endomorphs to recognition on incremental upgrades and have a good time small victories to preserve morale high.

Ultimately, at the same time as the endomorph diet and workout plan calls for cautious management, it's far by no means a sentence to negative health or obesity. With the proper techniques and a commitment to a wholesome life-style, endomorphs can gain and maintain a healthy weight and frame composition. This tailor-made approach now not most effective enhances their physical fitness however additionally boosts their intellectual well-being and excellent of existence.

Overview of somatotypes

Somatotypes are a class device used to categorize human frame types primarily based on their physiques and predispositions towards certain physical and metabolic traits. This concept was advanced within the Nineteen Forties by American psychologist William Herbert Sheldon, who described three number one somatotypes: ectomorph, mesomorph, and endomorph. Each type displays distinct tendencies and tendencies in body composition, metabolism, and personality, consistent with Sheldon's unique idea. In this evaluation, we can explore all three somatotypes with a special awareness on the endomorphic frame kind.

General Overview of the Three Somatotypes

Ectomorphs are characterised by using a narrow, linear appearance with little body fats and muscle. They usually have a tough time gaining weight due to a quick metabolism. Ectomorphs are often defined as tall and skinny, with narrow shoulders and hips. Mesomorphs showcase a greater muscular and properly-built physique. They have a herbal tendency to construct muscle and preserve a lower frame fat percentage. Mesomorphs are normally properly-proportioned and may benefit and shed pounds highly without difficulty, making them properly-suitable for power and electricity sports.

Endomorphs, the primary recognition of this dialogue, generally tend to have a better body fats percentage, with a huge amount of their mass saved within the decrease frame. They frequently struggle with weight control due to a slower metabolism. Endomorphs are generally shorter and have a rounder body shape with huge hips and shoulders.

The unique challenges and strengths of endomorphs

Endomorphs are one of the three body types labeled within the somatotype idea advanced by psychologist William Herbert Sheldon. The different sorts are ectomorphs and mesomorphs. Each body kind has particular traits that affect physical appearance, metabolism, and normal health. Endomorphs are usually characterized through a better percentage of frame fat, a rounder body, and a tendency to benefit weight without problems. This body kind faces particular challenges and possesses distinct strengths, which we can explore in detail.

Understanding Endomorphs

Understanding endomorphs requires a deep dive into their physiological, metabolic, and mental characteristics. By exploring these attributes, we are able to better recognize the unique challenges and strengths related to this body kind, and debunk common stereotypes that are neither correct nor beneficial.

Stereotypes and Misconceptions

Endomorphs are often subject to stereotypes that paint them as lazy or missing in area. These stereotypes stem from societal biases that equate thinness with virtue and fitness. However, frame kind and metabolism are largely encouraged through genetics, and the idea that endomorphs can without difficulty trade their frame composition with minimal attempt is each unrealistic and unfair. These misconceptions can result in enormous psychological misery, together with feelings of inadequacy, low vanity, and frame photo issues. It's important for society to understand that fitness can are available various sizes, and that each frame type has its own set of strengths and demanding situations.

In knowledge the endomorph frame kind, it is crucial to technique with a balanced angle that recognizes the inherent physiological developments whilst addressing the man or woman's holistic fitness desires. By doing so, endomorphs can optimize their fitness and nicely-being, leveraging their natural strengths and efficaciously dealing with their demanding situations. Moreover, dispelling stereotypes and embracing a more inclusive view of fitness and fitness can assist foster a extra supportive surroundings for all body kinds.

Strategies for Thriving as an Endomorph

To conquer challenges and leverage their strengths, endomorphs can undertake particular techniques:

1. Tailored Diet

A food plan decrease in carbohydrates and better in proteins and healthy fats can assist manage weight and metabolic issues. Portion manage and meal timing also are important.

2. Regular Exercise

A mixture of cardiovascular and energy training exercises can assist boost metabolism, construct muscle, and improve heart fitness. It's vital for endomorphs to discover fun activities to maintain consistency.

3. Professional Guidance

Consulting with nutritionists, personal running shoes, and scientific professionals can provide personalized advice and guide, assisting endomorphs acquire their fitness and health goals.

4. Psychological Support

Addressing the mental impact of being an endomorph thru counseling or help groups can beautify mental nicely-being and motivation.

For endomorphs, the key to a success weight loss and muscle advantage lies in expertise their frame's unique responses to food plan and exercise. Tailoring their techniques to meet those desires—focusing on a balanced, low-glycemic eating regimen, a aggregate of HIIT and strength training, and prioritizing sleep and strain control—can result in powerful and sustainable physical modifications. By embracing their precise physiological make-up and operating with it, instead of towards it, endomorphs can optimize their health and fitness effects.

Part I
UNDERSTANDING THE ENDOMORPHIC DIET

Chapter 1
FUNDAMENTALS OF ENDOMORPHIC NUTRITION

The concept of endomorphic vitamins revolves around the understanding and alertness of nutritional strategies tailor-made to individuals with an endomorphic body type. This body type, characterized by a better percentage of frame fat and a robust, rounded physique, requires unique dietary concerns to optimize health, control weight, and beautify normal properly-being. This comprehensive manual will delve into the fundamentals of endomorphic vitamins, exploring the physiological tendencies of endomorphs, best nutritional standards, and practical strategies to attain a balanced and healthy lifestyle.

Understanding the Endomorphic Body Type

Defining the Endomorphic Body Type

The endomorphic frame type is one of the 3 classifications in the somatotype spectrum that still includes ectomorphs and mesomorphs. Each kind has awesome bodily characteristics and metabolic profiles, influencing person dietary and workout needs. Endomorphs are frequently characterised through a better frame fat percentage, a extensive bone shape, and a smooth, spherical body composition. This frame kind can effortlessly gain fat and muscle, generally displaying a strong and strong body.

Characteristics:

- Higher Body Fat Percentage: Endomorphs generally tend to have a higher frame fats percent, which may be both a physiological trait and a project. This characteristic is due to a combination of genetic elements, metabolic performance, and hormonal affects, that may predispose endomorphs to store more fats than other frame kinds.
- Wide Bone Structure: A sturdy and extensive bone shape is another hallmark of the endomorphic body kind. This structural trait contributes to a normally larger physique and might effect the entirety from garb in shape to the types of bodily activities which can be maximum comfortable and effective.
- Propensity to Store Fat: Endomorphs are evidently inclined to keep strength within the shape of fats. This trait become in all likelihood high-quality in ancestral instances when meals shortage changed into common, however in modern plentiful meals surroundings, it could result in effortlessly gaining weight if not managed properly.

Common Challenges:

- Slower Metabolism: Endomorphs often experience a slower metabolic fee compared to different body kinds. This slower metabolism method that energy are burned at a slower pace, which could complicate efforts to lose weight.

- Difficulty in Losing Weight: Due to their gradual metabolism and efficient fats garage, endomorphs frequently discover it more challenging to shed pounds. This is specifically true whilst traditional diets are not tailored to their specific metabolic needs.
- Susceptibility to Certain Health Issues: The combination of better body fats, a propensity to shop fat, and a slower metabolism could make endomorphs more vulnerable to health problems consisting of type 2 diabetes, cardiovascular disease, and metabolic syndrome. Managing frame composition thru weight loss program and exercising is vital for decreasing these dangers.

Physiological Insights

Understanding the physiological underpinnings of the endomorphic body type can help tailor more effective health and fitness techniques.

Metabolic Considerations:

- Basal Metabolic Rate (BMR): BMR represents the range of energy required to maintain your body performing at rest. Endomorphs regularly have a lower BMR than would be predicted based on their frame mass, that means they burn fewer calories even as at rest compared to other frame types. This trait underscores the significance of changing caloric intake to actual metabolic price in place of popular calculators, which won't account for somatotype variations.
- Implications for Endomorphs: For endomorphs, information and adapting to their BMR is critical. It calls for precise modifications in nutritional consumption and physical hobby to create a caloric deficit for weight loss or to control weight efficaciously.

Hormonal Influences:

- Insulin Sensitivity: Insulin is a vital hormone in glucose metabolism and fats storage. Endomorphs frequently have various levels of insulin sensitivity, that could affect their frame's capability to utilize glucose and store fat. Lower insulin sensitivity can cause higher blood sugar levels and more fats garage, in particular if the diet is rich in high-glycemic carbohydrates.
- Other Hormonal Factors: Besides insulin, different hormones like cortisol (the strain hormone) and sex hormones additionally play big roles in weight control and body composition. For example, elevated cortisol degrees can exacerbate weight advantage in endomorphs, specially across the middle.

By delving into those characteristics and demanding situations, endomorphs can higher recognize how to manage their particular body kind thru tailor-made dietary and lifestyle changes. This expertise is step one closer to developing a customised method that complements health consequences and aligns with their specific physiological desires.

Nutritional Strategies for Endomorphs

Macronutrient Ratios

Understanding the stability of macronutrients—fat, proteins, and carbohydrates—is crucial for coping with the endomorphic body type efficiently. Macronutrients are the pillars of any weight loss plan, and for endomorphs, the balance among those vitamins can greatly impact their metabolic consequences. Fats, proteins, and carbohydrates every play particular roles in the frame, and striking the proper balance can assist control weight, optimize power tiers, and enhance standard fitness.

For endomorphs, it's far generally advocated to emphasise protein consumption, slight carbohydrate intake, and make certain a healthful consumption of fat. High protein intake is crucial as it enables in constructing and maintaining muscular tissues, that's essential in view that muscle groups burns greater energy than fats tissue. Proteins also have a excessive thermic effect, that means they burn more energy during digestion than different macronutrients.

Carbohydrates need to be consumed carefully. Since endomorphs can have a propensity to store fats more without difficulty, decrease carbohydrate intake allows save you spikes in blood sugar stages, which can cause fat garage. When consuming carbohydrates, the focus must be on complicated carbohydrates, which destroy down slowly and provide sustained strength with out the spikes in insulin levels.

Healthy fats are also important, in spite of not unusual misconceptions that fats are negative to weight control. Fats are essential for hormonal balance, which includes hormones that modify metabolism and appetite. The secret is to pick the proper varieties of fats, inclusive of the ones found in avocados, nuts, seeds, and fatty fish, that can help metabolism and decrease irritation.

Choosing the Right Carbohydrates

For endomorphs, deciding on the proper type of carbohydrates is especially important. Low-glycemic index ingredients are favored because they've a lesser effect on blood glucose stages. Foods like complete grains, legumes, and most end result and greens release glucose slowly into the bloodstream, providing extra sustained energy and minimizing insulin spikes. This controlled release enables in handling appetite and decreasing the likelihood of fats garage.

Fiber-wealthy meals also play a vital function inside the diet of an endomorph. Foods excessive in fiber, including oats, apples, pears, and green leafy greens, now not only help in keeping decrease blood sugar stages however additionally growth satiety. This feeling of fullness can save you overeating and assist in dealing with overall calorie intake, which is beneficial for weight manage. Fiber additionally supports digestive health with the aid of supporting to preserve ordinary bowel moves and may assist in lowering levels of cholesterol.

Protein's Pivotal Role

Protein is mainly pivotal for endomorphs because of its a couple of roles in frame composition management, metabolism, and satiety. The satisfactory types of proteins for endomorphs consist of lean meats like hen breast and turkey, plant-based proteins which includes lentils and chickpeas, and coffee-fats dairy products. These proteins provide essential amino acids without excessive calories from fat. Moreover, protein has a great thermogenic impact, which means it requires greater energy for digestion, absorption, and disposal than fats or carbohydrates. This expanded energy expenditure can help enhance metabolic rate, that's often slower in endomorphs. Additionally, protein consumption enables in muscle preservation and growth, which is vital because muscle tissue plays a key position in metabolic rate.

Healthy Fats: Types and Benefits

Understanding the sorts of fats and their advantages is vital for endomorphs. Saturated fats, located in ingredients like butter and red meat, ought to be limited, while monounsaturated and polyunsaturated fat have to be integrated into the weight loss program. Monounsaturated fats, found in olive oil, avocados, and positive nuts, help with weight manage and reduce the risk of heart sickness. Polyunsaturated fats, which include omega-three fatty acids found in fish like salmon and mackerel, are crucial for lowering infection and helping mind and coronary heart health.

Omega-three fatty acids, especially, are anti inflammatory and may assist counteract the infection frequently related to obesity and metabolic syndrome. These fat also play a position in regulating leptin, a hormone involved in hunger and metabolism regulation. Balancing the consumption of these wholesome fats can cause better health effects for endomorphs through supporting metabolic capabilities and lowering disorder chance elements related to better body fat ranges. By that specialize in those dietary techniques, endomorphs can tailor their eating regimen to higher suit their physiological needs, selling more effective weight control and average health improvements.

Dietary Patterns and Meal Planning

Meal Frequency and Timing

The dietary styles of an character, particularly someone with an endomorphic frame type, significantly have an impact on their metabolic health and normal health. One issue that calls for cautious consideration is the frequency and timing of meals. Traditionally, most dietary plans revolve round 3 important meals according to day. However, for endomorphs, who tend to have a slower metabolism, eating common, smaller meals may be greater beneficial. This approach can help in regulating blood sugar degrees, keeping steady strength ranges all through the day, and stopping the acute starvation that can lead to overeating.

The timing of meals also plays a important role in optimizing metabolic responses. Eating at ordinary durations can assist stabilize insulin tiers and decrease fluctuations in blood glucose. For endomorphs, it's far normally recommended to eat a balanced meal or snack each three to four hours. This sample can also sell better nutrient usage and save you the frame from coming into a catabolic kingdom, wherein muscle breakdown takes place. In the evening, it can be positive to consume in advance instead of later, as metabolism commonly slows down as one prepares for sleep. An early dinner ensures that the frame has ample time to digest the meal before bedtime, thus assisting in weight control and metabolic health.

Portion Control and Caloric Intake

Effective element manage is a fundamental detail in dealing with weight, mainly for endomorphs, who are vulnerable to gaining weight without problems. One beneficial approach is the use of smaller plates or bowls, that could certainly encourage smaller servings. Visual cues also can play a substantial function; as an instance, filling half of of the plate with veggies, a quarter with lean proteins, and the closing region with entire grains can help ensure a balanced intake without the want to matter calories meticulously.

Understanding and dealing with caloric intake also are important. Endomorphs normally have a lower basal metabolic rate, this means that they burn fewer energy at relaxation as compared to people with other body types. It is essential for endomorphs to have a clean information of their caloric desires, which can be calculated primarily based on factors consisting of age, sex, weight, top, and level of bodily hobby. This expertise permits them to tailor their meals consumption more precisely to aid their metabolism with out ingesting excess energy, that may cause weight benefit.

Hydration and Its Overlooked Importance

Hydration is another crucial, even though regularly omitted, issue of effective nutritional planning for endomorphs. Water performs a key function in keeping metabolic health and assisting in weight management. It is concerned in severa bodily functions, consisting of digestion and the transport of vitamins. Adequate water consumption facilitates to make sure that the metabolic techniques, inclusive of lipolysis, the breakdown of fats, occur efficiently.

For endomorphs, who may will be predisposed for maintaining fluids, consuming an adequate amount of water also can help in decreasing water weight and bloating. The widespread advice for water intake is ready eight eight-ounce glasses in keeping with day, but this could range based totally on character needs, environmental situations, and tiers of bodily pastime. It's useful to drink water always in the course of the day, and specifically essential to hydrate before, at some stage in, and after workout routines to support restoration and efficient calorie burn.

Understanding and imposing powerful meal making plans and nutritional styles are important for endomorphs aiming to manage their weight and improve their metabolic health. By specializing in meal frequency and timing, practising element manipulate, and making sure ok hydration, endomorphs can create a sustainable approach to eating that helps their frame type and complements their usual nicely-being.

Integrating Physical Activity with Nutritional Efforts

Understanding a way to effectively combine bodily interest with dietary efforts is vital for individuals with an endomorphic frame kind. This integration paperwork the cornerstone of a holistic approach to health, focusing no longer handiest on what is consumed however additionally on how the body uses those vitamins via physical interest. The synergy between weight-reduction plan and exercise can lead to advanced frame composition, higher metabolic fitness, and an typical growth in nicely-being.

Synergy Between Diet and Exercise

The dating among eating regimen and exercise is specifically massive for endomorphs, who can also struggle with weight management and metabolic efficiency. A nicely-deliberate weight loss plan can fuel the frame for greatest overall performance during workouts, whilst the right forms of physical activity can enhance the body's metabolic rate, assisting in more effective use of dietary nutrients. For endomorphs, the key's to discover a stability that promotes fats loss at the same time as keeping lean muscle groups. By combining a nutrient-dense, managed-calorie food regimen with a strategic exercise routine, endomorphs can create a metabolic environment conducive to weight loss and stepped forward health.

Types of sporting activities that supplement dietary efforts for endomorphs

For endomorphs, selecting the right sort of exercising is as important as the eating regimen they follow. Strength schooling is especially recommended as it helps build muscle mass, which in turn will increase the basal metabolic charge (BMR). Muscle tissue burns more calories than fat tissue, even at rest, which may be a giant advantage in weight control. Incorporating complete-frame workout routines or compound actions including squats, deadlifts, and bench presses may be mainly powerful.

In addition to power schooling, cardiovascular workout is critical for burning energy and improving heart health. However, in place of long, slow, and steady cardio sessions, high-intensity interval education (HIIT) is probably greater powerful for endomorphs. HIIT entails short bursts of excessive exercising alternated with low-depth recovery intervals, which has been shown to burn more fats and decorate metabolic health more notably than consistent-kingdom cardio. This type of schooling can also be less time-eating and may fit extra easily into a busy schedule.

The impact of energy training and cardiovascular sporting activities on body composition

The impact of combining energy schooling with cardiovascular exercising may be profound on frame composition. Strength training will increase muscular tissues, elevating the variety of energy burned at relaxation, while cardiovascular workout burns calories and facilitates lessen body fat. This dual technique not simplest allows in reducing frame fats percentage but also improves normal body power and cardiovascular staying power. For endomorphs, who certainly have a higher frame fat percentage, this blended method can drastically adjust frame composition in a high quality manner, main to a leaner and greater toned physique.

Routine and Consistency

Developing a constant ordinary is pivotal in the journey to reaching and maintaining top-quality fitness. For endomorphs, consistency in both food regimen and workout can help mitigate the natural tendency towards gaining weight and might foster sustainable behavior. A recurring does now not mean sticking rigidly to a particular set of meals or workout routines however rather setting up a normal pattern that fits into one's way of life and can be adapted as needed.

The importance of adaptability and being attentive to the body's cues

While consistency is important, similarly vital is the potential to be adaptable. Listening to the frame's cues is crucial for adjusting dietary intake and exercising routines to match contemporary health status, strength ranges, and other life occasions. Endomorphs, mainly, may also locate that their bodies reply otherwise to certain meals or varieties of workout at extraordinary times. For example, all through periods of pressure or hormonal changes, the frame may not reply as predicted to a formerly effective ordinary. Being open to tweaking and refining each dietary and workout plans ensures persisted progress closer to health dreams.

Moreover, adaptability enables in handling plateaus or setbacks in weight loss trips, which are common amongst endomorphs. By being flexible and attentive to the body's wishes, people can conquer these hurdles greater efficiently and maintain motivation and commitment to their fitness and fitness dreams. This approach no longer most effective improves physical health however additionally supports intellectual and emotional well-being, creating a more balanced and sustainable life-style for those with an endomorphic frame kind.

Macronutrient ratios: The stability among protein, fat, and carbohydrates.

Understanding the balance among protein, fat, and carbohydrates is critical for all and sundry trying to enhance their health, manage their weight, or optimize their bodily performance. Each macronutrient plays a completely unique function within the frame, and finding the right stability can help achieve various health goals. This complete exploration into macronutrient ratios will shed light at the features of proteins, fats, and carbohydrates, and provide steering on the way to efficaciously balance those to fulfill person dietary desires.

The Role of Proteins in Nutrition

Proteins are fundamental components of all dwelling cells and are crucial for building and repairing tissues, helping immune characteristic, and contributing to a sense of fullness. They are made from amino acids, which are the constructing blocks for maximum systems and capabilities in the frame. Including good enough protein within the weight loss program can assist hold muscular tissues, particularly essential in weight control and growing old.

The Impact of Fats on Health

Fats have regularly been misunderstood, but they may be crucial to human fitness. They offer strength, aid cellular growth, guard organs, and assist maintain the frame warm. Fats also resource within the absorption of a few nutrients and the manufacturing of crucial hormones. Dietary fat are labeled into saturated, unsaturated, and trans fats, each having distinctive effects on fitness. Understanding the differences between these can substantially impact disorder hazard and overall health.

Carbohydrates as Energy Sources

Carbohydrates are the frame's fundamental supply of electricity. They are damaged down into glucose, that is used to fuel cells, tissues, and organs. Carbohydrates may be simple or complicated, impacting blood sugar degrees and fitness differently. The first-class and quantity of carbohydrates consumed can have an effect on weight control, electricity degrees, and metabolic fitness.

Finding the Right Macronutrient Balance

The most suitable stability of protein, fats, and carbohydrates can vary extensively based on an man or woman's age, intercourse, interest degree, and fitness goals. For instance, athletes may require greater carbohydrates for power, even as the ones trying to lose weight may benefit from growing protein intake. Understanding how to adjust those ratios can cause better fitness outcomes and advanced bodily performance.

Effects of Macronutrient Manipulation on Metabolism

Adjusting macronutrient ratios can have an impact on the metabolism. A eating regimen higher in protein and fat, with decrease carbohydrates, for instance, can cause ketosis, a country wherein the frame turns into fantastically green at burning fat for electricity. On the alternative hand, excessive-carbohydrate diets can aid intense bodily hobby and faster healing instances. Each macronutrient has a one of a kind impact on satiety, metabolic rate, and hormonal responses, that could affect how energy are burned and saved.

Personalizing Macronutrient Ratios for Weight Management

One of the primary motives people regulate their macronutrient ratios is for weight management. High-protein diets can reduce urge for food and increase feelings of fullness. At the equal time, moderate to high fats consumption can also sell satiety. Balancing those with carbohydrates that offer sustained strength can save you overeating and guide weight reduction or preservation.

Macronutrients and Disease Prevention

Beyond weight control, the stability of macronutrients can affect various fitness results, together with the threat of developing diseases like kind 2 diabetes, coronary heart sickness, and certain cancers. Diets with a balanced consumption of top notch macronutrients can assist lengthy-time period fitness and decrease disease hazard.

Challenges in Balancing Macronutrients

Despite the advantages, balancing macronutrients can be difficult. Common obstacles include misjudging element sizes, not knowledge the macronutrient content material of ingredients, and nutritional regulations or preferences that make it difficult to achieve a stability. Education, planning, and every so often running with a nutrition professional can assist triumph over these challenges.

The balance among protein, fat, and carbohydrates is not a one-length-fits-all equation. It requires personalization based totally on person health wishes, life-style, and dreams.

By know-how the jobs and results of every macronutrient, individuals can make informed decisions about their diets and enhance their overall fitness and nicely-being. Adjusting macronutrient ratios may be a powerful device in coping with health and optimizing bodily overall performance, making it a crucial element of nutrition science.

Importance of dietary fiber and hydration

Dietary fiber and hydration play pivotal roles in keeping standard fitness, but they're regularly neglected in each day nutrition. Fiber is essential for digestive fitness, cardiovascular well being, and even weight control, while right hydration is important for certainly every physical feature. Understanding the impact of these nutritional components can extensively enhance one's quality of life.

Dietary Fiber: A Cornerstone of Health

Fiber, a non-digestible carbohydrate observed in plant meals, has profound advantages on various elements of fitness. It is available in paperwork: soluble and insoluble, each serving particular features within the body. Soluble fiber dissolves in water to shape a gel-like substance, helping to decrease glucose levels and cholesterol. Insoluble fiber, on the other hand, affords bulk to stool and aids in shifting food through the digestive machine, preventing constipation.

The benefits of a excessive-fiber eating regimen amplify past digestion. It has been linked to decreased risks of growing heart disease, diabetes, and bowel cancer. Fiber-wealthy ingredients like fruits, vegetables, legumes, and whole grains naturally make consuming a fulfilling revel in, regularly followed by way of a decrease calorie consumption and prolonged satiety. This can be mainly useful for weight management. Additionally, the fermentation of some fibers within the colon produces brief-chain fatty acids which can provide electricity to colon cells and help keep colon fitness.

Hydration: Essential for Life

Hydration is similarly important for health. Water is the frame's most important chemical aspect, making up about 60% of frame weight. Every machine inside the body depends on water to feature. It flushes pollution from the important organs, carries nutrients to cells, affords a moist surroundings for ear, nostril, and throat tissues, and gets rid of waste. The significance of hydration extends to bodily overall performance and cognitive feature, influencing the entirety from staying power and strength to concentration and temper. Dehydration can be a severe issue and manifests thru diverse signs and symptoms together with thirst, decreased urine output, dry skin, fatigue, mild-headedness, and darkish-colored urine. Chronic dehydration can cause extra extreme health issues like kidney stones, hypertension, and urinary tract infections.

Fiber and Hydration: A Synergistic Relationship

The courting among nutritional fiber and hydration is synergistic, in particular regarding digestive health. While fiber will increase the majority of the stool and speeds its passage thru the intestine, water enables soften the stool, reducing the risk of constipation. This interaction highlights the importance of consuming enough fluids whilst growing dietary fiber. Adequate hydration is necessary to maximize the benefits of a excessive-fiber weight-reduction plan and prevent capacity negative side results inclusive of intestinal discomfort and constipation.

Impact of Fiber and Hydration on Chronic Diseases

Fiber and proper hydration are effective tools in opposition to persistent diseases. For instance, excessive-fiber diets are associated with a lower hazard of cardiovascular disease due to their ability to reduce both blood stress and levels of cholesterol. The hydration status impacts blood viscosity and blood stress. Regular consumption of fiber and maintaining hydration also can play roles in the prevention and control of type 2 diabetes. Fiber improves blood sugar manage, while adequate hydration can also have an impact on glucose metabolism and help prevent the disorder.

Cognitive and Emotional Benefits

Emerging studies shows that fiber and hydration may have cognitive and emotional advantages. Adequate hydration has been proven to preserve cognitive performance, in particular in children and the elderly, even as fiber affects gut fitness, that is intently connected to intellectual health through the intestine-mind axis. Diets better in fiber can lead to lower fees of depression and anxiety, probably due to the advanced intestine microbiota health.

Practical Tips for Incorporating More Fiber and Water into the Diet

Incorporating greater fiber into the weight loss plan can be as simple as selecting entire fruits over juices, choosing complete grains in place of refined, and increasing the intake of greens and legumes. To improve hydration, sporting a reusable water bottle and ingesting water-wealthy ingredients like cucumbers, celery, and watermelon can assist. The importance of nutritional fiber and hydration can't be overstated. They are essential to preserving health and stopping sickness. By making easy nutritional changes to boom the consumption of fiber and water, individuals can revel in profound health advantages that enlarge from physical to intellectual properly-being.

Chapter 2
FOODS TO PREFER AND TO AVOID

Endomorphs regularly face particular challenges in managing their weight and retaining a wholesome metabolism. To deal with these demanding situations, a diet wealthy in particular vitamins and tailored to their physiological wishes can be extremely beneficial. This article gives an extensive listing of ingredients that are appropriate for individuals with an endomorphic frame kind, aiming to resource in weight control, decorate metabolism, and aid normal fitness.

Proteins for Satiety and Metabolic Boost

Lean Meats: High-pleasant proteins are critical for the endomorphic diet, supporting to enhance metabolism and provide lengthy-lasting satiety. Lean meats which includes chook breast, turkey, and lean cuts of pork are brilliant selections. These meats are low in fat however high in protein, which allows in constructing lean muscle tissues and enhancing metabolic fee. For people who decide on variety, other lean meats like venison and bison offer comparable benefits with a unique taste profile.

- Fish: Omega-three fatty acids, crucial for reducing inflammation and assisting heart health, are abundantly discovered in fatty fish. Salmon is famend for its excessive omega-3 content and its capacity to help cardiovascular fitness. Mackerel and sardines are also extremely good sources, presenting notable protein and important fats that may improve lipid profiles and increase brain health. For range, incorporating fish like herring or trout also can improve the eating regimen with omega-three fatty acids and other essential vitamins.
- Eggs: As a powerhouse of nutrition, eggs provide not most effective superb protein but additionally an amazing stability of crucial amino acids. They are flexible in cooking and can be blanketed in diverse meals in the course of the day, from breakfast scrambles to protein-packed salads or snacks. The yolks are rich in nutrients, minerals, and antioxidants, which guide overall fitness and power.
- Plant-Based Proteins: For people who pick plant-primarily based diets or want to include greater plant-primarily based food, lentils, chickpeas, and black beans are valuable. These legumes aren't handiest excessive in protein however additionally comprise enormous amounts of fiber, which facilitates regulate blood sugar tiers and promotes a sense of fullness. Tofu, tempeh, and edamame are soy-based proteins which are staples in vegetarian and vegan diets, regarded for their high protein content material and flexibility in numerous recipes, from stir-fries to smoothies.

Fiber-Rich Vegetables and Fruits

Leafy Greens: Spinach, kale, and Swiss chard are loaded with vitamins and minerals at the same time as being very low in calories. These veggies can assist improve metabolic fitness and are easy to contain into diets, whether or not in smoothies, salads, or as a cooked aspect dish.

Cruciferous Vegetables: Broccoli, cauliflower, and Brussels sprouts aren't best excessive in fiber however also comprise compounds which can help decorate the body's cleansing techniques and help metabolic health. These greens may be roasted, steamed, or stir-fried, making them flexible additions to food.

Other Vegetables: Bell peppers, cucumbers, and zucchini are low-calorie vegetables that provide crucial vitamins without including extra calories. These may be used in salads, as a part of a vegetable stir-fry, or honestly snacked on with hummus or other healthy dips.

Berries and Fruits: Berries like raspberries, blueberries, and strawberries are wealthy in antioxidants and occasional in glycemic load, making them best for coping with blood sugar tiers. They are best for a quick snack, a fiber-rich addition to breakfasts, or as a natural sweetener in desserts. Apples and pears comprise soluble fiber that aids digestion and facilitates maintain steady blood sugar stages.

Whole Grains and Low-Glycemic Carbohydrates

Incorporating complete grains and coffee-glycemic carbohydrates into an endomorph's food regimen is essential for keeping power stages, regulating blood sugar, and helping overall health. Beyond the well-known options like oats, quinoa, and brown rice, there are several other nutritious selections which can diversify the diet while providing vital advantages.

Comprehensive List of Suitable Whole Grains and Carbohydrates:

- Oats: Known for their heart-healthy properties and ability to stabilize blood glucose ranges, oats are versatile and may be utilized in breakfast cereals, smoothies, and baking.
- Quinoa: A whole protein containing all 9 vital amino acids, quinoa is likewise gluten-loose and rich in fiber, making it an fantastic choice for a filling meal.
- Brown Rice: Less processed than white rice, brown rice retains its natural fibers, vitamins, and minerals, assisting digestive fitness and providing sustained electricity.
- Barley: This grain is specifically excellent for coronary heart health because of its excessive fiber content, and it additionally allows manage blood sugar tiers, making it best for diabetics or those dealing with their weight.
- Bulgur: Known for its position in Middle Eastern delicacies, bulgur is a quick-cooking whole grain that is high in fiber and protein, with a nutty taste that complements a whole lot of dishes.
- Farro: An historical grain with a chewy texture and rich, nutty taste, farro is packed with fiber, protein, and antioxidants. It's awesome in salads, soups, and stews.
- Sweet Potatoes: As a root vegetable, candy potatoes offer a low-glycemic carbohydrate alternative that is wealthy in fiber, vitamins A and C, and antioxidants. They can be baked, roasted, or mashed.

- Amaranth: This lesser-recognized grain is gluten-free and excessive in protein, fiber, and micronutrients such as magnesium and iron, making it a nutritious addition to any meal.

Healthy Fats for Hormonal Balance and Satiety

Healthy fats are pivotal in regulating hormone degrees, decreasing irritation, and providing lengthy-lasting satiety, that may resource weight management. For endomorphs, together with assets of monounsaturated and polyunsaturated fat can assist stability metabolic functions and guide normal health.

Comprehensive List of Foods High in Healthy Fats:

- Avocados: A versatile source of monounsaturated fat, avocados can be used in salads, smoothies, or as a range on toast. They're additionally rich in fiber and potassium.
- Nuts and Seeds: Almonds, walnuts, flaxseeds, and chia seeds are not handiest high in healthful fats however also provide protein, fiber, and crucial nutrients like omega-3 fatty acids, that are crucial for heart and brain fitness.
- Olive Oil: A staple inside the Mediterranean weight-reduction plan, olive oil is outstanding for dressing salads, drizzling over cooked vegetables, or as a base for sauces. It's rich in antioxidants and monounsaturated fats.
- Coconut Oil: Suitable for cooking at high temperatures, coconut oil provides a source of medium-chain triglycerides (MCTs), recognized for their ability to boost metabolic charge and offer brief electricity.
- Walnuts: These nuts aren't simplest suitable for heart health however also provide a significant quantity of omega-three fatty acids, which might be useful for decreasing infection.
- Pumpkin Seeds: Rich in magnesium, zinc, and fatty acids, pumpkin seeds are a brilliant snack that allows keep hormone balance and supports heart fitness.

Dairy and Dairy Alternative

For endomorphs, dealing with calorie intake while making sure ok nutrient density of their meals is important. Dairy products and their options can play a huge role on this balancing act.

- Greek Yogurt: This thick, creamy yogurt isn't always most effective decrease in lactose because of the straining method but also full of protein, that may assist in muscle preservation and satiety. It's a flexible food that can be utilized in smoothies, as a base for dressings, or without a doubt enjoyed with a sprinkle of nuts and berries for a nutritious snack.
- Cottage Cheese: With its excessive protein content material and occasional fat alternatives, cottage cheese is great for endomorphs aiming for weight loss or muscle gain. It can be eaten plain, brought to salads, or combined into smoothies to growth protein consumption with out notably raising energy.
- Skim Milk: For individuals who can tolerate dairy, skim milk offers an awesome supply of protein and calcium without the fats content of complete milk. It may be used in cereals, espresso, and tea or used as a base for protein-wealthy smoothies.
- Almond Milk: As a dairy alternative, unsweetened almond milk is low in energy and

fat whilst presenting a respectable amount of calcium and vitamin E, a powerful antioxidant. It's a extraordinary choice for those on a plant-primarily based food regimen or with lactose intolerance.
- Soy Milk: Rich in protein and fortified with vitamins and minerals, soy milk is a more in-depth dietary fit to cow's milk than other plant-based options. It's beneficial for those seeking to boom their protein intake while also getting critical vitamins like calcium and diet D.
- Oat Milk: Another incredible dairy alternative, in particular for those with nut and soy allergic reactions. Oat milk is better in carbohydrates than different milk options however gives a creamy texture and useful fibers, making it a heart-healthy choice.

Herbs, Spices, and Condiments

Utilizing herbs, spices, and condiments can rework simple components into flavorful meals without adding immoderate energy or unhealthy additives. This is specially useful for endomorphs, who need to keep their food thrilling even as dealing with caloric consumption.

- Cinnamon: Known for its ability to assist adjust blood sugar tiers, cinnamon is a spice that may be added to the entirety from espresso and oatmeal to yogurt and fruit. This makes it a valuable addition to the endomorphic eating regimen, supporting to govern cravings and insulin spikes.
- Turmeric: With its active component curcumin, turmeric is well known for its anti-inflammatory homes. Adding turmeric to food can help reduce inflammation, which is essential for people with a better body fat percentage as adipose tissue can contribute to continual low-level infection.
- Ginger: Another spice with powerful anti-inflammatory properties, ginger can also help with digestion and nausea. It's versatile within the kitchen, suitable for flavoring everything from stir-fries and soups to teas and smoothies.
- Parsley: This herb is not handiest a taste enhancer however also rich in vitamins A and C, as well as antioxidants. It's ideal for garnishing dishes or adding to inexperienced juices and smoothies for an extra nutrient kick.
- Cilantro: Known for its exceptional flavor, cilantro is wealthy in diet K, which is important for bone health. It additionally has detoxifying houses, which can be useful for retaining liver health and universal health.
- Basil: Aromatic and flavorful, basil gives more than just a flavor enhancement to dishes; it's additionally an excellent source of magnesium, which plays a role in over three hundred enzymatic reactions in the body, which includes those worried in strength metabolism.

Common nutritional pitfalls and the way to keep away from them

Many individuals locate themselves unwittingly falling into commonplace dietary pitfalls which could preclude their development. Understanding these pitfalls and learning strategies to avoid them is vital for lengthy-time period achievement and accomplishing surest health. This article explores the maximum frequent dietary mistakes and gives realistic advice to dodge those common mistakes.

Misunderstanding Portion Sizes

One of the maximum prevalent problems in weight-reduction plan is the misunderstanding of element sizes. It's clean to underestimate the quantity of food we eat, main to unintentional overeating. To fight this, people can use measuring gear like cups, scales, or even their palms as rough gauges to govern portions correctly. Visual cues also can be helpful, consisting of equating a serving of meat to the scale of a deck of cards. Recognizing the suitable portions can make a considerable distinction in dietary fulfillment.

Skipping Meals

Many humans trust that skipping food will help them lose weight. However, this exercise can cause expanded hunger and overeating later within the day. It's important to preserve a normal eating time table to stabilize blood sugar ranges and manage hunger. Instead of skipping food, choose smaller, nutrient-dense meals that encompass a stability of protein, fats, and carbohydrates.

Choosing Processed Foods Over Whole Foods

Processed ingredients are often handy and cheap, but they're typically low in vitamins and excessive in energy, fats, sugars, and sodium. These foods can cause weight benefit and health problems through the years. To keep away from this pitfall, focus on incorporating extra entire meals like culmination, veggies, complete grains, and lean proteins into your weight loss program. These ingredients aren't only greater nutritious however also offer extra satiety which allows control urge for food.

Not Reading Labels Properly

Many clients do no longer pay enough attention to meals labels, lacking essential records about calorie content, serving length, and nutrient amounts. It's essential to read labels carefully to make informed food selections. Pay particular attention to the serving size and the quantity of servings in step with container, as this could be misleading.

Overconsumption of "Healthy" Foods

Just because a meals is classified as "healthful" does no longer suggest it is low in energy or can be eaten in massive portions. Foods like nuts, avocados, and olive oil are healthful however calorie-dense. Consuming those meals sparsely is prime to keeping a balanced food plan.

Neglecting Liquid Calories

Drinks like sodas, juices, and even specialty coffees can comprise a giant quantity of energy and sugars. These liquid calories upload up fast and might sabotage weight loss efforts. It's really helpful to limit sugary drinks and choose water, natural teas, or black coffee instead.

Relying on Dining Out

Eating out often could make it hard to control what goes into your meals and how it is prepared. Restaurant meals are regularly higher in energy and sodium than home-cooked food. To keep away from this pitfall, try to cook more food at domestic wherein you could control the ingredients and cooking strategies. When eating out, opt for grilled or steamed dishes instead of fried alternatives, and ask for dressings or sauces on the side.

Failing to Plan

Failure to plan is one in every of the biggest dietary pitfalls. Without a meal plan, you're much more likely to make negative food alternatives out of convenience or desperation. Planning meals and snacks in advance of time guarantees that you have healthful options to be had while you want them. It additionally helps with grocery purchasing and reduces meals waste.

Ignoring Hunger Cues

Ignoring the body's herbal hunger cues can lead to overeating or consuming the wrong varieties of foods. It's crucial to listen on your frame and devour whilst you're absolutely hungry. Conversely, understand when you're eating out of boredom, stress, or emotion, and discover different approaches to deal with the ones feelings.

Part II
BEYOND DIET AND EXERCISE

Chapter 3
HOLISTIC LIFESTYLE CHANGES FOR ENDOMORPHS

When it involves coping with the endomorph body type, food regimen and nutrition play a pivotal position. The unique physiological characteristics of endomorphs, inclusive of a propensity to save fat and a slower metabolism, necessitate a considerate approach to what they eat and when they eat. Let's delve into the important thing elements of an optimum eating regimen for endomorphs, focusing on macronutrient balance, meal frequency, and hydration.

Diet and Nutrition for Endomorphs

Macronutrient Balance

The basis of an effective food regimen for endomorphs lies in reaching the right balance of macronutrients: proteins, carbohydrates, and fat. Each plays a crucial function in coping with frame composition and usual fitness.

- Protein: For endomorphs, high protein intake is essential. Proteins have a high thermogenic effect and may significantly increase metabolism, making them an critical thing of weight control. They also assist to reduce urge for food and extend feelings of fullness, which is in particular useful for endomorphs who may enjoy extra common starvation. Furthermore, proteins are vital for muscle renovation and growth. Muscles not simplest improve frame composition however also increase metabolic charge, assisting in more efficient calorie burning. Sources of terrific protein encompass lean meats which include bird breast, turkey, and lean cuts of pork. Fish which include salmon and mackerel offer omega-three fatty acids at the side of protein, that may assist reduce inflammation and guide metabolic fitness. For vegetarians or the ones trying to lessen meat consumption, plant-primarily based proteins like lentils, chickpeas, and quinoa are extremely good selections. These meals offer not most effective protein however also fiber, which can in addition resource in urge for food manage and insulin control.

- Carbohydrates: Managing carbohydrate consumption is important for endomorphs due to their impact on insulin tiers and the body's tendency to shop fat. Opting for low to moderate carbohydrate intake can help mitigate these troubles. It is critical to attention on carbohydrates with a low glycemic index, which have a slower effect on blood glucose degrees. Foods together with complete grains, non-starchy veggies, and maximum fruits fall into this class. These carbohydrates provide sustained electricity without the giant insulin spikes that cause fats garage. Furthermore, they may be wealthy in fiber, which aids in digestion and extended satiety, assisting to keep away from overeating.
- Fats: While frequently vilified in eating regimen subculture, fats are vital for hormonal balance and typical health. They play a critical role in nutrient absorption, brain function, and satiation. For endomorphs, incorporating healthy fat into the weight loss plan can help to modify starvation and resource in lengthy-time period weight management. Sources of healthy fat consist of avocados, which can be also rich in potassium and fiber, nuts and seeds, which give protein and fiber along with fats, and olive oil, that is high in monounsaturated fats acknowledged to aid coronary heart health. It is critical to mild fats consumption, however, as fat are calorie-dense and immoderate consumption can without difficulty cause calorie surplus.

Frequent, Smaller Meals

For endomorphs, the traditional 3 huge meals an afternoon won't be the handiest technique. Eating smaller, greater common food can assist maintain a extra strong blood sugar degree, reducing the chance of great insulin spikes that sell fat storage. This eating sample also can help manage starvation, lessen calorie intake, and increase the efficiency of metabolism in the course of the day. Ideally, these food should be properly-balanced, containing an excellent blend of protein, fats, and occasional-glycemic carbohydrates to ensure sustained energy and satiety.

Hydration

Hydration is any other critical thing of weight loss plan for endomorphs. Water plays a critical role in metabolism and helps in the processing and burning of calories. It is likewise crucial for digestion and may assist prevent overeating through contributing to a sense of fullness. For endomorphs, who might also have a slower metabolism, staying effectively hydrated is crucial for reinforcing metabolic rate and helping in weight control. The well-known recommendation of eight glasses of water per day is a great starting point, but desires can range primarily based on character elements together with pastime stage, climate, and universal fitness. In addition to water, eating liquids like inexperienced tea can be beneficial because of its metabolism-boosting antioxidants.

A well-based food regimen wealthy in nutrients and balanced in macronutrients, blended with an appropriate meal frequency and ok hydration, can considerably have an impact on the fitness and weight control efforts of an endomorph. This holistic technique to nutrients not handiest allows in achieving and preserving an most beneficial weight however also supports typical metabolic health, that's critical for long-term wellness.

Exercise and Physical Activity

Maintaining an lively way of life is vital for endomorphs, who have a tendency to gain weight effortlessly and have a slower metabolism. By focusing at the right mix of cardiovascular exercising, strength schooling, and flexibility paintings, endomorphs can optimize their body composition and general health. Here's an in depth guide on how every workout class can be tailored to gain endomorphs, entire with unique sporting activities and practical pointers.

1. Cardiovascular Exercise

Cardiovascular exercising is vital for all and sundry seeking to improve their coronary heart fitness and calorie expenditure. For endomorphs, it's mainly crucial as it enables to offset their slower metabolic rate.

Key Cardio Exercises:

a. **High-Intensity Interval Training (HIIT):**

Exercise: Sprint Intervals

INSTRUCTIONS
- After a warm-up of mild jogging for five mins
- dash at maximum attempt for 30 seconds followed through 1 minute of walking or gradual strolling to get better.
- Repeat for 20 mins.

Tips: Ensure right hydration earlier than starting and wear footwear that offer accurate ankle assist to prevent accidents.

Indoor Cycling

Exercise:

- Interval Cycling

INSTRUCTIONS USE AN INDOOR CYCLING MOTORBIKE
- start at a slight tempo for five mins
- Then trade between 1 minute of high-depth biking and 2 mins at a slight pace.

- Continue for half-hour.

Tips: Adjust the seat height to avoid knee strain. Focus on preserving a clean pedaling form.

Rowing

Exercise: Rowing Machine Intervals

INSTRUCTIONS
- Start with a five-minute mild row accompanied via units of 2-minute high-depth rowing and 1 minute of mild rowing for restoration.
- Repeat for 30 minutes.

Tips: Keep your again instantly and use your legs for electricity to reduce the strain for your back.

Stair Climbing

Exercise: Stair Sprinting

INSTRUCTIONS
- Find a fixed of stairs or use a stair gadget.
- Sprint up the steps as rapid as feasible and stroll down slowly for restoration.
- Repeat for 15-20 mins.

Tips: Focus on pushing through your legs and keeping balance to enhance energy and safety.

Jump Rope

Exercise: Jump Rope Intervals

INSTRUCTIONS
- Start with 30 seconds of speedy jump roping accompanied by means of 30 seconds of rest.
- Repeat for 15-20 mins.

Tips: Use a weighted leap rope to growth the intensity, and make certain the rope is the right duration in your peak.

Strength Training

Strength schooling is essential for growing muscle groups, that could assist improve basal metabolic charge (BMR), allowing endomorphs to burn greater calories even even as at relaxation.

Key Strength Exercises

a. Squats:

Exercise: Barbell Squat

INSTRUCTIONS
- Stand with ft hip-width apart
- Conserving a barbell throughout your upper returned.

ENDOMORPH DIET AND EXERCISE PLAN / 31

- Bend knees and decrease right into a squat while retaining your back immediately.
- Return to the begin.
- Perform 3 units of 10 reps.

Tips: Keep your chest up and push through your heels to upward push for max efficiency and protection.

b. Deadlifts:

Exercise: Conventional Deadlift

INSTRUCTIONS
- Stand with toes shoulder-width aside
- a barbell in front of you.
- Bend and grip the barbell, arise with the aid of lifting the bar
- keeping it close to your frame.
- Lower it backpedal.
- Do three units of eight reps.

Tips: Keep your again straight and lift the use of your legs and hips to prevent lower back accidents.

c. Bench Press:

Exercise: Flat Bench Press

INSTRUCTIONS
- Lie on a bench with a barbell above your chest.
- Lift the bar off the rack
- slowly decrease it in your chest
- and press it up
- Perform 3 units of 10 reps.

Tips: Use a spotter for protection and to help you raise heavier weights properly.

d. Pull-Ups:

Exercise: Assisted Pull-Up

INSTRUCTIONS
- Use an assisted pull-up device or resistance band for help if needed.
- Perform pull-united states of americathrough lifting your frame up until your chin is above the bar, then decrease slowly.
- Do 3 units of eight reps.

Tips: Focus on a complete range of motion and managed movements to maximize muscle engagement.

e. Leg Press

Exercise: Leg Press Machine

INSTRUCTIONS
- Sit on a leg press machine with toes on the platform
- Push the platform away the use of your legs, then slowly return to the starting role
- Perform 3 sets of 10 reps.

Tips: Do no longer lock your knees on the top of the movement to keep anxiety for your leg muscle tissue and protect your joints.

Flexibility and Mobility Work

Flexibility and mobility physical activities help hold joint fitness, enhance muscle elasticity, and decrease pressure, which may be in particular useful for endomorphs who need pressure reduction to control weight gain.

Key Flexibility Exercises

a. Yoga

Exercise: Sun Salutation

INSTRUCTIONS
- Perform a series of poses that waft smoothly into every other
- Together with upward and downward canine
- Ahead bend, and mountain pose.
- Complete at least five cycles.

Tips: Focus on deep, managed respiratory to decorate rest and versatility.

b. Pilates

Exercise: The Hundred

INSTRUCTIONS
- Lie in your back, raise your legs to a tabletop role
- Improve your head and shoulders
- And pump your palms whilst breathing deeply for a hundred beats.

Tips: Engage your core during the exercising to Improve posture and center energy.

c. Dynamic Stretching

Exercise: Leg Swings

INSTRUCTIONS
- Hold onto a solid floor
- swing one leg ahead and backward
- progressively growing the variety of movement.
- Perform 20 swings in keeping with leg.

Tips: Keep your higher body strong to isolate the motion in your legs.

Static Stretching

Exercise: Seated Forward Bend

INSTRUCTIONS
- Sit with legs extended
- inhale, and as you exhale
- lean forward out of your hips
- achieving for your feet.
- Hold for 30 seconds.
- Repeat two times.

Tips: Do now not spherical your back; aim to lengthen your backbone as you fold forward.

e. Foam Rolling

Exercise: Foam Roll for Legs

INSTRUCTIONS
- Use a foam roller below your thighs, calves, and glutes.
- Slowly roll to and fro to massage and release muscle tightness.

Tips: Spend more time on tight regions however keep away from rolling at once on joints or bones.

Incorporating these tailored workout strategies will assist endomorphs no longer best improve their physical health however also raise their metabolism and enhance their ordinary well-being. Consistency is prime, and it's vital to combine those physical activities with a balanced food regimen and true life-style behavior for nice outcomes.

Stress Management and Sleep

Stress Reduction: Understanding the Impact of Stress on Endomorphs

For endomorphs, stress can exacerbate weight benefit due to their frame's tendency to save fat. When stressed, the frame produces excess cortisol, a hormone that now not handiest contributes to fat garage however additionally makes fats loss in particular difficult. High cortisol stages can growth appetite and cravings for excessive-fats, high-sugar foods, main at once to weight advantage, that is mainly tricky for endomorphs who evidently have a slower metabolism.

Effective Stress-Management Techniques

MEDITATION

Meditation is a effective tool for reducing pressure. Regular exercise facilitates to quiet the mind, lessen cortisol tiers, and enhance universal emotional resilience. For endomorphs, a every day meditation practice may be a cornerstone of strain management, helping in the discount of compulsive consuming behaviors and enhancing intellectual readability and awareness.

Deep Breathing Exercises

Deep respiratory is every other powerful pressure reduction method that can be practiced anywhere at any time. Techniques like diaphragmatic breathing (deep belly respiratory) assist to activate the frame's parasympathetic fearful system, promoting rest and lowering stages of pressure hormones. For endomorphs, integrating deep respiration into day by day routines, mainly for the duration of moments of high strain or when cravings strike, can help control instantaneous strain responses and support long-term health desires.

Mindfulness and Mindful Eating

Mindfulness involves staying present and fully enticing inside the current moment. Applying mindfulness to ingesting can assist endomorphs end up greater attuned to their hunger and satiety cues, stopping overeating. By eating mindfully, they can revel in their food extra very well, apprehend whilst they are complete, and keep away from pointless calorie consumption, which is important for dealing with frame weight.

Yoga

Yoga, which regularly includes each meditative and bodily factors, can be particularly useful for strain discount. Regular yoga exercise improves flexibility, strength, and pressure levels. For endomorphs, yoga not simplest allows in handling stress however also contributes to physical interest goals, which are important for weight control and metabolic health.

Adequate Sleep

The Importance of Sleep for Endomorph

Sleep plays a crucial position in metabolic health, hormonal balance, and average physical and mental nicely-being. Lack of ok sleep can disrupt hormonal balances, consisting of those of cortisol and insulin, which control pressure and blood sugar ranges, respectively. For endomorphs, making sure enough exceptional sleep is vital for maintaining a healthful metabolism, decreasing cravings, and minimizing the danger of insulin resistance and kind 2 diabetes.

Strategies for Enhancing Sleep Quality

Consistent Sleep Schedule

Maintaining a consistent sleep schedule enables adjust the frame's inner clock, leading to improved sleep fine. Endomorphs ought to purpose to visit bed and wake up on the same time every day, even on weekends, to guide their circadian rhythms.

Optimizing Sleep Environment

Creating a nap-conducive environment is critical for excellent quality sleep. This consists of a groovy, darkish, and quiet bed room. Investing in snug bedding and minimizing mild and noise pollutants can appreciably improve sleep first-rate. Additionally, doing away with digital gadgets from the bed room can lessen sleep disturbances and the temptation to engage with screens earlier than bedtime.

Pre-sleep Routine

A relaxing pre-sleep habitual can help sign to the frame that it's time to wind down. This would possibly include activities like analyzing, taking a warm tub, or mild stretching. Avoiding stimulants including caffeine and extreme physical hobby near bedtime is likewise vital for endomorphs to attain restful sleep.

Managing Sleep Disorders

Endomorphs experiencing sleep issues together with insomnia or sleep apnea need to are seeking professional medical recommendation. Addressing these disorders is critical for enhancing sleep great and ordinary health. Treatments can also include life-style modifications, clinical interventions, or behavioral therapy.

For endomorphs, coping with stress and making sure good enough, restful sleep aren't just supplementary aspects of a wholesome lifestyle; they are relevant additives that extensively influence their success in achieving and preserving a healthy weight and metabolism. By enforcing effective stress control strategies and optimizing sleep, endomorphs can decorate their standard health, nicely-being, and satisfactory of life, setting a solid foundation for different fitness-promoting practices in their holistic life-style method.

The importance of constant and sustainable way of life changes

The importance of steady and sustainable life-style modifications is more and more identified in our speedy-paced, current global. With the growing occurrence of continual illnesses, mental health issues, and environmental issues, the need for a holistic method to fitness and sustainability has in no way been more crucial. Embracing life-style modifications which might be both steady and sustainable can profoundly effect our private properly-being, network fitness, and the global surroundings.

Lifestyle adjustments encompass a whole lot of practices that aim to improve an man or woman's fitness, nicely-being, and effect on the arena. These adjustments can include modifications in weight-reduction plan, exercise, stress control, and environmental consciousness. One of the primary advantages of imposing such modifications is the improvement in overall physical fitness. Regular bodily hobby and a balanced weight loss program can save you the onset of persistent sicknesses such as obesity, diabetes, and coronary heart ailment. Moreover, constant exercising and healthy eating can enhance mental fitness, decreasing signs and symptoms of melancholy and anxiety, and improving mood and cognitive function.

The advantages of way of life modifications amplify past the individual. By adopting extra sustainable habits, people contribute to wider network and environmental health. For instance, selecting regionally sourced and plant-based totally ingredients can reduce carbon footprints and help local economies. Similarly, minimizing waste and holding strength within households can have a widespread advantageous impact on the surroundings, contributing to the reduction of world warming and pollution.

Despite these blessings, keeping consistency in lifestyle changes can be hard. The key to sustainability lies in placing realistic dreams and integrating changes progressively into every day life. It is essential for individuals to select modifications that in shape their unique existence and preferences to avoid burnout and make sure lengthy-term adherence. Additionally, social assist from circle of relatives, buddies, and community individuals can play a critical role in motivating individuals to maintain these changes.

Technology and present day conveniences can both prevent and assist the pursuit of a sustainable lifestyle. While era can lead to sedentary behaviors and elevated consumption, it may additionally provide tools and sources that assist wholesome behavior. Mobile apps that tune vitamins, exercising, and mental health can assist people reveal their development and live on course. Likewise, online groups and boards can offer treasured guide and information that encourage sustained life-style changes.

Government rules and societal systems additionally play critical roles in supporting or impeding sustainable life-style adjustments. Urban making plans that promotes walkable cities, availability of public recreational regions, and accessibility to healthy meals can facilitate physical interest and better consuming behavior. Conversely, a lack of regulatory assist for environmental sustainability tasks can undermine man or woman efforts. Therefore, advocacy for rules that aid health and sustainability on the network and national stages is essential.

The impact of regular and sustainable way of life changes is likewise glaring within the place of job. Companies that sell healthy conduct and environmental responsibility not most effective improve their personnel' health but also beautify their own reputations and efficiency. Such projects can cause reduced healthcare prices, expanded productivity, and a extra encouraged staff. Employers can play a pivotal role via creating environments that inspire sustainable practices, consisting of providing wholesome meal options and enabling flexible paintings preparations to reduce commuting pressure.

Education is any other important detail in fostering sustainable way of life modifications. By integrating fitness and environmental schooling into faculty curriculums from an early age, children can increase recognition and habits that final an entire life. Educating the younger era approximately the significance of sustainability and fitness no longer most effective blessings individual students however additionally promotes a more fit and greater environmentally aware society within the destiny.

The significance of steady and sustainable way of life changes is multifaceted and a long way-accomplishing. These adjustments provide considerable advantages for person fitness, community nicely-being, and global environmental health. Achieving sustainability in life-style modifications requires realistic goal-placing, slow integration of practices, community assist, and supportive policies and academic systems. As individuals, communities, and societies, fostering those adjustments is not just beneficial however imperative for a more fit and extra sustainable global.

Part III
THE 30-DAY FOOD PLAN

Chapter 3
BASICS OF MEAL PLANNING

The idea of meal making plans for an endomorph eating regimen is focused on understanding the particular metabolic and physical traits of the endomorph frame type. Endomorphs are commonly characterised by means of a higher percentage of body fats, a slower metabolism, and a more tendency to advantage weight. This makes them particularly aware of a cautiously controlled food regimen and a structured eating plan. The intention of meal planning for endomorphs is to promote fats loss, hold muscle tissues, and enhance average metabolic health. This involves a mixture of macronutrient management, caloric manage, and strategic meal timing.

Macronutrient Ratios

Understanding and handling macronutrient consumption is vital for endomorphs, who generally have a slower metabolism and a better body fat percentage. The balanced consumption of macronutrients—proteins, carbohydrates, and fat—isn't simplest pivotal for weight management however also for normal metabolic fitness. This stability enables endomorphs to mitigate the danger of fats accumulation, enhance muscle upkeep, and stabilize electricity stages for the duration of the day.

Protein and Its Critical Role inside the Endomorph Diet

For endomorphs, protein is an vital aspect of the weight loss plan. Its significance extends beyond simply muscle maintenance and growth; protein additionally possesses a excessive thermic effect. This approach that it requires greater strength for digestion, absorption, and disposal than different macronutrients, which allows in burning more calories. Therefore, incorporating a better percentage of protein within the weight-reduction plan can clearly decorate the metabolic rate, that's useful for weight management.

A higher intake of protein also contributes to expanded feelings of fullness, which could assist lessen average caloric intake via curbing the desire to snack on unhealthy alternatives. For endomorphs, it's far endorsed that protein constitutes approximately 30-forty% of the full caloric consumption. This can be accomplished through the inclusion of lean meats together with hen and turkey, fish wealthy in omega-3 fatty acids like salmon and trout, low-fats dairy products, eggs, legumes, and a whole lot of plant-primarily based proteins inclusive of tofu and tempeh. These protein sources no longer handiest help muscle increase and repair but also contribute to a sustained release of electricity, retaining endomorphs satiated and active during the day.

The Importance of Selecting the Right Carbohydrates

Carbohydrates are often considered with warning in endomorph eating regimen plans because of the body kind's propensity in the direction of insulin sensitivity. This sensitivity can result in extended fats garage if now not managed well. Therefore, selecting the right sort of carbohydrates is important. Low-glycemic carbohydrates, which have a minimum impact on blood sugar tiers, are preferred. These sorts of carbs encompass foods like complete grains, non-starchy veggies, and a few culmination that don't purpose a dramatic spike in insulin stages.

Incorporating approximately 30-forty% of carbohydrates into the food regimen is recommended, and timing their consumption can also play a important function in managing insulin sensitivity. Consuming carbohydrates around bodily sports—while the frame is more likely to apply glucose as gas in preference to storing it as fats—can be a strategic approach for endomorphs. This approach ensures that carbohydrates are utilized for healing and strength throughout and after workouts rather than contributing to accelerated fats garage.

Fats: Ensuring Hormonal Balance and Satiety

While fat may be high in energy, they are critical for hormonal stability and can extensively useful resource in prolonging emotions of fullness. For endomorphs, integrating healthy fats into the diet is critical, and that they have to goal for these fats to make up approximately 30% of their nutritional consumption. Sources of beneficial fats include avocados, which can be wealthy in monounsaturated fat; nuts and seeds, which provide a combination of monounsaturated and polyunsaturated fats such as omega-3 fatty acids; olive oil; and fatty fishes consisting of salmon and mackerel.

The inclusion of healthful fats inside the weight loss plan now not best supports metabolic functions and cardiovascular fitness however also contributes to a extra regulated urge for food. By improving satiety, healthy fats prevent overeating and can assist manage caloric consumption without the feeling of deprivation that often accompanies weight-reduction plan.

Balancing Macronutrients for Optimal Results

The control of macronutrients calls for a considerate technique that mixes knowledge of vitamins with an understanding of one's personal frame responses. For endomorphs, the balance of macronutrients should be adjusted to house their unique metabolic wishes and desires. It's additionally vital to recollect the satisfactory of the macronutrients selected—no longer all proteins, carbs, and fat are created equal in phrases of their health advantages and effects on frame composition.

Regular monitoring and adjustment of macronutrient ratios are beneficial, as they are able to exchange with variations in metabolic price, activity degree, and weight loss progress. Consulting with a dietitian or a nutritionist can provide customized steering to assist endomorphs make informed selections about their food regimen, making sure that they acquire all of the necessary vitamins even as nonetheless promoting fat loss and muscle maintenance.

The strategic control of macronutrient intake paperwork the muse of a a hit endomorph weight-reduction plan. By that specialize in incredible proteins, low-glycemic carbohydrates, and healthy fat, endomorphs can enhance their metabolic health, enhance frame composition, and reap their weight management desires greater successfully. This balanced approach no longer only supports brief-term achievement however also promotes long-term health and well-being.

Planning Meal

In the world of meal planning, especially for those with an endomorph body type, preserving variety and balance to your food regimen is important. A nicely-notion-out meal plan can drastically have an effect on your metabolic fitness, weight management, and normal nicely-being. Below, we delve deeper into how to successfully plan meals for breakfast, lunch, dinner, and snacks, emphasizing fantastic components, nutritional balance, and catering to the specific wishes of an endomorph.

Breakfast: Setting the Metabolic Tone for the Day

Breakfast is regularly referred to as the maximum essential meal of the day, and for an awesome motive. For endomorphs, beginning the day with a meal that is excessive in protein and fiber can help kickstart the metabolism and hold satiety throughout the morning. A vegetable omelette, as an example, packs a effective punch of protein from the eggs and a fiber-wealthy array of vitamins from veggies like spinach, mushrooms, and peppers. This combination helps regulate blood sugar degrees and keeps hunger pangs at bay. Another incredible breakfast option is Greek yogurt combined with nuts and berries. Greek yogurt is a high-quality source of protein and probiotics, which might be beneficial for digestive health. Berries add a low-glycemic index sweetness and are loaded with antioxidants, while nuts provide wholesome fats and a satisfying crunch.

Protein smoothies also are an top notch choice for an on-the-cross breakfast. A combination of whey or plant-based protein powder, a handful of greens like kale or spinach, a few frozen berries, and a small portion of avocado for smoothness can create a scrumptious, nutrient-packed drink that sustains energy levels well into the day.

Lunch and Dinner: Sustaining Energy with Balanced Meals

For lunch and dinner, specializing in lean proteins, a mild quantity of healthful fats, and a wealth of greens can assist endomorphs manipulate weight and optimize fitness. A usual lunch may consist of grilled hen served over a bed of blended greens dressed lightly with olive oil and lemon juice. This meal is not only filling but additionally offers a extensive spectrum of vitamins including iron, nutrition C, and vital fatty acids. Salmon, another extremely good protein source, may be paired with asparagus for dinner. This fish is rich in omega-3 fatty acids, which can be essential for heart health and cognitive features. Asparagus, then again, is a powerhouse of fiber, folate, and nutrients A, C, and K. Together, they offer a meal this is as scrumptious as it is nutritious.

For people who enjoy red meat, a beef stir-fry with lots of vegetables which includes bell peppers, broccoli, and snap peas can be a awesome addition to the eating regimen. Beef offers remarkable protein and iron, at the same time as the vegetables bring in fiber, vitamins, and antioxidants that assist fight irritation and bolster health.

Snacks: Smart Choices for Sustained Energy

Snacks are essential to any healthy dietweight-reduction plan as they assist manage starvation among meals and provide an extra strength enhance. For an endomorph, it's critical that snacks are thoughtfully chosen to keep away from useless sugar spikes and caloric overload. Hummus and carrots make a exceptional snack mixture—hummus provides both protein and fiber, even as carrots are excessive in beta-carotene and different essential nutrients. An apple with a small amount of peanut butter is some other splendid snacking desire. The apple affords fiber and a candy crunch, whilst the peanut butter adds a dose of protein and healthy fat, making it a fulfilling mini-meal that could assist reduce cravings and save you overeating at meal times.

A handful of almonds is a simple yet powerful snack for the ones busy days while you need something short and nourishing. Almonds are rich in nutrition E, calcium, magnesium, and potassium, making them an super snack for maintaining power tiers and supporting metabolic health.

Setting your self up for success

Creating a functional and efficient kitchen starts with information the necessities. This does not simply imply buying the proper gear, but additionally knowing the way to store accurately for them. Whether you're a novice prepare dinner or a person seeking to revamp your kitchen, putting your self up for achievement may be honest in case you observe some guided principles.

The first step to a well-prepared kitchen is having a terrific set of knives. A chef's knife, a paring knife, and a serrated bread knife cowl maximum reducing obligations you'll come upon from dicing vegetables to slicing bread. Look for high-carbon chrome steel knives as they offer durability and simplicity of sharpening. Investing in a nice knife sharpener is similarly essential to hold the edge and performance of your knives.

Another foundational device is a robust reducing board. Consider having at the least: one for produce and the other for uncooked meats, hen, and seafood to prevent pass-infection. Materials like bamboo or tough maple are durable and offer a great stability between hardness and gentleness on knives. Cookware is any other critical category. A set that consists of as a minimum one large and one small saucepan, a deep sauté pan, and a massive stockpot can take care of maximum cooking desires. Cast iron skillets are prized for his or her warmness retention and flexibility—terrific for searing meats or baking cornbread. Non-stick pans are important for sensitive tasks like cooking eggs or pancakes.

When it involves baking, a great first-rate sheet pan, a rectangular baking dish, a loaf pan, and a spherical cake pan may be used for an array of recipes. Invest in heavy-gauge metallic pans that don't warp and offer even warmness distribution. Now, bear in mind the smaller but quintessential gear such as a set of dry and liquid measuring cups, measuring spoons, a whisk, a vegetable peeler, and a grater. These equipment may additionally seem minor but play a essential position inside the precision that cooking requires. Add a couple of timber spoons, a spatula, and a ladle, and your primary toolkit is complete.

With tools sorted, allow's communicate about shopping for kitchen essentials. The rule of thumb is to shop for the exceptional you may afford, but always look for value. High rate doesn't always suggest high first-rate. Read critiques, ask for hints, and take a look at merchandise if possible. Look for gadgets with strong warranties and precise customer service. When purchasing for kitchen equipment, timing can also play a tremendous role in snagging the quality deals. Major sales frequently occur round holidays and change of seasons. Also, recollect touring restaurant supply shops, which offer professional high-quality at aggressive costs and are open to the public.

The identical thoughtfulness applies to grocery buying. Planning is vital. Start by means of making plans your food for the week earlier than you buy groceries. This will not best shop money and time however also lessen meals waste. Stick on your shopping listing but stay flexible if you find proper deals on perishables that you can use in specific meals. Understanding seasons is prime to shopping for produce. Seasonal fruits and veggies now not handiest taste better but are also inexpensive whilst they are in abundance. Also, don't shy away from shopping for frozen end result and veggies, which may be just as nutritious as their sparkling opposite numbers and last a great deal longer. Buying in bulk can store money however be careful—buy larger portions most effective of items you operate frequently and have a protracted shelf lifestyles. For perishables like meats, divide them into meal-length quantities and freeze what you don't want at once. Another tip is to put money into correct garage solutions for your meals. Quality airtight packing containers maintain your food brisker for longer and help keep your pantry prepared. Labels may be helpful to mark dates on spices and other perishables.

Lastly, consider your dietary behavior and alternatives. If you observe a specific food plan or have nutritional restrictions, ensure your kitchen is stocked with the necessities that cater to those desires. Whether it's dairy-loose alternatives, gluten-free flours, or plant-based totally protein sources, having those items with no trouble available will make meal preparation easier and make certain you persist with your dietary dreams. Setting up your kitchen with the right equipment and getting to know to save well for both equipment and groceries can remodel your cooking enjoy from irritating to gratifying. With this foundation, you're no longer just geared up however additionally empowered to prepare dinner with self belief and ease, making your kitchen a cornerstone of your each day achievement.

Chapter 4
WEEK-THROUGH-WEEK GUIDE

Day 1

Breakfast: Spinach and Feta Omelette

INGREDIENTS
- 3 massive eggs
- 1 cup fresh spinach, chopped
- 1/four cup feta cheese, crumbled
- 1 tbsp olive oil
- Salt and pepper to flavor

INSTRUCTIONS
- Heat olive oil in a skillet over medium warmness.
- Sauté spinach till wilted, about 2 minutes.
- Beat the eggs and pour over the spinach. Cook for approximately 2 mins or until the eggs begin to set.

- Sprinkle feta cheese on pinnacle and fold the omelette in half of. Cook for another 2 minutes.
- Season with salt and pepper, serve hot.

Timing: 10 minutes
Tips: Ensure the skillet is well heated earlier than adding eggs to save you sticking.

Lunch: Turkey and Avocado Wrap

INGREDIENTS
- 1 entire wheat wrap
- four oz.Turkey breast, sliced
- half avocado, sliced
- 1/four cup combined veggies
- 2 tbsp Greek yogurt
- Salt and pepper to flavor

INSTRUCTIONS
- Lay the wrap flat on a plate.
- Spread Greek yogurt over the wrap.
- Add turkey slices, avocado, and mixed veggies.
- Season with salt and pepper.
- Roll the wrap tightly and reduce in half.

Timing: 5 mins
Tips: Use lean turkey breast to hold the fats content in test.

Dinner: Grilled Salmon with Asparagus

INGREDIENTS
- 6 ozsalmon fillet
- 1 tbsp olive oil
- 1 garlic clove, minced
- 1 tbsp lemon juice
- 1 cup asparagus, ends trimmed
- Salt and pepper to taste

INSTRUCTIONS
- Preheat grill to medium-excessive.
- Rub salmon with olive oil, garlic, and lemon juice. Season with salt and pepper.
- Grill salmon for approximately 6 minutes according to aspect or till cooked via.
- Simultaneously, grill asparagus for approximately five mins, turning now and again.
- Serve salmon and asparagus warm.

Timing: 20 mins
Tips: Let the salmon relaxation for a few minutes after grilling to enhance juiciness.

Snack: Greek Yogurt and Berries

INGREDIENTS
- 1 cup Greek yogurt, plain
- half cup blended berries (blueberries, strawberries)
- 1 tbsp honey

INSTRUCTIONS
- In a bowl, integrate Greek yogurt and combined berries.
- Drizzle honey on pinnacle.

Timing: 2 minutes
Tips: Opt for full-fats Greek yogurt for better satiety and flavor.

Day 2

Breakfast: Almond Butter Banana Smoothie

INGREDIENTS
- 1 banana
- 2 tbsp almond butter
- 1 cup almond milk
- 1 scoop vanilla protein powder

INSTRUCTIONS
- Combine all ingredients in a blender.
- Blend till smooth.

Timing: five minutes
Tips: Add a handful of spinach for additonal nutrients with minimum flavor alternate.

Lunch: Chicken Salad with Olive Oil Dressing

INGREDIENTS
- four ouncesgrilled bird breast, chopped
- 1 cup blended greens
- 1/4 cucumber, sliced
- 1/four purple onion, thinly sliced
- 2 tbsp olive oil
- 1 tbsp balsamic vinegar
- Salt and pepper to flavor

INSTRUCTIONS
- In a big bowl, integrate veggies, cucumber, and onion.
- Top with grilled chicken.
- In a small bowl, whisk together olive oil, balsamic vinegar, salt, and pepper.
- Drizzle dressing over the salad.

Timing: 10 mins
Tips: Prepare the chicken in advance to save time.

Dinner: Beef Stir-Fry with Broccoli

INGREDIENTS
- 6 ozlean pork strips
- 1 cup broccoli
- florets
- half of bell pepper, sliced
- 2 tbsp soy sauce
- 1 tbsp sesame oil
- 1 garlic clove, minced
- 1 tsp ginger, grated

INSTRUCTIONS
- Heat sesame oil in a big skillet over medium-excessive heat.
- Add garlic and ginger; sauté for 1 minute.
- Add pork strips; cook dinner until browned, about 5 minutes.
- Add broccoli and bell pepper; cook dinner till veggies are gentle, about five mins.
- Stir in soy sauce and cook dinner for another 2 minutes.

Timing: 15 mins
Tips: Slice red meat thinly to make sure brief or even cooking.

Snack: Cottage Cheese and Pineapple

INGREDIENTS
- 1/2 cup cottage cheese
- 1/2 cup pineapple chunks

INSTRUCTIONS
- Mix cottage cheese with pineapple chunks in a bowl.

Timing: 2 minutes
Tips: Choose low-fats cottage cheese for a healthier choice.

Day 3

Breakfast: Chia Seed Pudding with Coconut Milk

INGREDIENTS
- 1/4 cup chia seeds
- 1 cup coconut milk
- 1 tbsp honey
- half of tsp vanilla extract

- Fresh berries for topping

INSTRUCTIONS
- In a bowl, mix chia seeds, coconut milk, honey, and vanilla extract.
- Cover and refrigerate in a single day.
- Serve crowned with clean berries.

Timing: Overnight (prep time 5 minutes)
Tips: Stir the mixture some times in the first hour to help distribute the chia seeds lightly.

Lunch: Quinoa and Black Bean Salad

INGREDIENTS
- 1/2 cup quinoa, cooked
- 1/2 cup black beans, rinsed and drained
- 1/4 cup corn kernels
- 1/4 crimson bell pepper, diced
- 2 tbsp cilantro, chopped
- 1 lime, juiced
- 1 tbsp olive oil
- Salt and pepper to taste

INSTRUCTIONS
- In a huge bowl, integrate quinoa, black beans, corn, crimson bell pepper, and cilantro.
- In a small bowl, whisk collectively lime juice, olive oil, salt, and pepper.
- Pour dressing over the salad and toss to combine.

Timing: 20 minutes
Tips: This salad can be made in advance and stored within the fridge for quick lunches.

Dinner: Lemon Garlic Tilapia with Zucchini

INGREDIENTS
- 2 tilapia fillets
- 2 tbsp olive oil
- 2 garlic cloves, minced
- 1 lemon, juiced and zested
- 1 zucchini, sliced into half of-moons
- Salt and pepper to flavor

INSTRUCTIONS
- Preheat over to 400°F (2 hundred°C).
- Place tilapia on a baking sheet. Drizzle with 1 tbsp olive oil and 1/2 the lemon juice, sprinkle with garlic, lemon zest, salt, and pepper.
- Toss zucchini with the last olive oil and lemon juice, arrange round tilapia.
- Bake for approximately 15 minutes, till fish is cooked via and zucchini is gentle.

Timing: 25 mins

Tips: Ensure the tilapia is not overlapped to cook dinner evenly.

Snack: Almonds and Dark Chocolate

INGREDIENTS
- 1/four cup almonds
- 1 ouncesdark chocolate (as a minimum 70% cocoa)

INSTRUCTIONS
- Combine almonds and darkish chocolate in a small bowl or bag for an on-the-go snack.

Timing: 1 minute
Tips: This snack is best for a fast electricity boost and enjoyable sweet cravings healthily.

Day 4

Breakfast: Greek Yogurt Smoothie with Spinach and Berries

INGREDIENTS
- 1 cup Greek yogurt
- half of cup blended berries (blueberries, raspberries)
- half cup spinach
- half of banana
- 1 tbsp flaxseed
- half of cup water or almond milk

INSTRUCTIONS
- Place all components in a blender.
- Blend until clean.

Timing: 5 mins
Tips: Add the beverages first to help the blender run greater smoothly.

Lunch: Turkey Chili

INGREDIENTS
- 1 lb ground turkey
- 1 onion, chopped
- 2 garlic cloves, minced
- 1 can diced tomatoes
- 1 can kidney beans, tired and rinsed
- 2 tbsp chili powder
- 1 tsp cumin
- half of cup water

- Salt and pepper to flavor

INSTRUCTIONS
- In a massive pot, sauté onion and garlic until translucent.
- Add ground turkey and cook till browned.
- Stir in tomatoes, kidney beans, chili powder, cumin, and water. Bring to a boil.
- Reduce warmness and simmer for 20 minutes.
- Season with salt and pepper.

Timing: 35 mins
Tips: Serve with a dollop of Greek yogurt for added creaminess and protein.

Dinner: Baked Cod with Sweet Potato Fries

INGREDIENTS
- 2 cod fillets
- 1 tbsp olive oil
- 1 tsp paprika
- 2 candy potatoes, peeled and cut into fries
- Salt and pepper to taste

INSTRUCTIONS
- Preheat oven to 425°F (220°C).
- Toss candy potato fries with half the olive oil and paprika. Arrange on a baking sheet and bake for 20 minutes.
- Season cod with salt, pepper, and closing paprika. Place on a baking sheet, drizzle with ultimate olive oil.
- Add cod to the oven with the fries. Bake for 15 minutes, until cod is flaky.

Timing: 35 minutes
Tips: Ensure the sweet potato fries aren't overcrowded at the baking sheet to get them crispy.

Snack: Celery Sticks with Peanut Butter

INGREDIENTS
- three celery sticks, reduce into 3-inch portions
- 2 tbsp herbal peanut butter

INSTRUCTIONS
- Spread peanut butter on celery sticks.

Timing: five mins
Tips: This is a super crunchy snack that offers both protein and wholesome fat.

Day 5

Breakfast: Avocado Toast with Poached Eggs

INGREDIENTS
- 2 slices complete grain bread
- 1 avocado, mashed
- 2 eggs
- Salt and pepper to flavor

INSTRUCTIONS
- Toast the bread slices to your liking.
- Spread mashed avocado lightly on each slice of toast.
- Poach the eggs in simmering water for approximately three-four mins.
- Place a poached egg on each slice of avocado toast.
- Season with salt and pepper.

Timing: 10 mins
Tips: Add a sprinkle of pink pepper flakes for an extra kick.

Lunch: Grilled Chicken Caesar Salad

INGREDIENTS
- 1 chicken breast, grilled and sliced
- 2 cups Romaine lettuce, chopped
- 1/four cup Parmesan cheese, shaved
- 2 tbsp Caesar dressing, low-fats
- Salt and pepper to flavor

INSTRUCTIONS
- Toss Romaine lettuce with Caesar dressing in a massive bowl.
- Top with sliced grilled chicken and Parmesan cheese.
- Season with salt and pepper.

Timing: 15 minutes
Tips: For a more healthy version, use Greek yogurt primarily based Caesar dressing.

Dinner: Shrimp and Vegetable Stir-Fry

INGREDIENTS
- 1 lb shrimp, peeled and deveined
- 1 cup broccoli florets
- 1 pink bell pepper, sliced
- 1 zucchini, sliced
- 2 tbsp soy sauce
- 1 tbsp sesame oil

- 1 garlic clove, minced

INSTRUCTIONS
- Heat sesame oil in a big skillet over medium-high heat.
- Add garlic and sauté for 1 minute.
- Add shrimp and vegetables. Stir-fry for about 5-7 mins until shrimp are purple and vegetables are gentle.
- Drizzle with soy sauce and stir nicely.

Timing: 20 minutes
Tips: Serve over a small part of brown rice or quinoa if desired.

Snack: Hummus with Carrot Sticks

INGREDIENTS
- 1/2 cup hummus
- 1 cup carrot sticks

INSTRUCTIONS
Serve carrot sticks with hummus for dipping.

Timing: 2 mins
Tips: Make your own hummus by means of blending chickpeas, tahini, lemon juice, and garlic for a more energizing, no-additive snack.

Day 6

Breakfast: Berry Protein Smoothie

INGREDIENTS
- 1 cup mixed berries (strawberries, blueberries, raspberries)
- 1 scoop protein powder (vanilla or unflavored)
- 1 cup almond milk
- 1 tbsp chia seeds

INSTRUCTIONS
Blend all ingredients until easy.

Timing: five mins
Tips: Freeze the berries earlier for a thicker, chillier smoothie.

Lunch: Lentil Soup

INGREDIENTS
- 1 cup lentils, rinsed
- 1 onion, chopped
- 2 carrots, diced

- 2 celery stalks, diced
- 1 can diced tomatoes
- four cups vegetable broth
- 1 tsp thyme
- Salt and pepper to taste

INSTRUCTIONS
- In a big pot, sauté onions, carrots, and celery until smooth.
- Add lentils, tomatoes, vegetable broth, and thyme. Bring to a boil.
- Reduce warmth and simmer for 30-35 minutes, until lentils are gentle.
- Season with salt and pepper.

Timing: 50 minutes
Tips: This soup may be made in huge batches and saved in the freezer for future meals.

Dinner: Turkey Meatballs with Zucchini Noodles

INGREDIENTS
- 1 lb ground turkey
- 1 egg, beaten
- 1/4 cup breadcrumbs
- 1/four cup Parmesan cheese, grated
- 1 garlic clove, minced
- 1 tsp Italian seasoning
- 2 zucchinis, spiralized
- 1 cup marinara sauce

INSTRUCTIONS
- Preheat oven to 375°F (one hundred ninety°C).
- In a bowl, mix floor turkey, egg, breadcrumbs, Parmesan, garlic, and Italian seasoning.
- Form into meatballs and place on a baking sheet.
- Bake for 20-25 mins, until cooked via.
- Serve meatballs over spiralized zucchini, crowned with marinara sauce.

Timing: forty minutes
Tips: Ensure the meatballs are uniformly sized to cook evenly.

Snack: Greek Yogurt with Honey and Walnut

INGREDIENTS
- 1 cup Greek yogurt
- 1 tbsp honey
- 1/4 cup walnuts, chopped

INSTRUCTIONS
Top Greek yogurt with honey and chopped walnuts.

Timing: 2 mins

Tips: Opt for full-fat Greek yogurt for extra fulfilling fats that help manipulate starvation.

Day 7

Breakfast: Oatmeal with Almond Butter and Banana

INGREDIENTS
- half cup rolled oats
- 1 cup almond milk
- 1 banana, sliced
- 1 tbsp almond butter

INSTRUCTIONS
- Cook oats in almond milk in step with package deal instructions.
- Stir in almond butter, top with sliced banana.

Timing: 10 mins
Tips: Add a sprinkle of cinnamon for introduced flavor without more energy.

Lunch: Grilled Veggie and Hummus Wrap

INGREDIENTS
- 1 whole wheat wrap
- 1/2 cup hummus
- 1/four cup grilled veggies (zucchini, bell pepper, onion)
- 1/4 avocado, sliced
- Salt and pepper to taste

INSTRUCTIONS
- Spread hummus at the wrap.
- Layer grilled veggies and avocado slices.
- Season with salt and pepper, roll tightly.

Timing: 10 minutes
Tips: Grill extra vegetables when making dinner for an clean lunch prep tomorrow.

Dinner: Baked Chicken with Roasted Brussels Sprouts

INGREDIENTS
- 2 chook breasts
- 1 tbsp olive oil
- 1 tsp garlic powder
- 1 lb Brussels sprouts, halved
- Salt and pepper to flavor

INSTRUCTIONS
- Preheat oven to four hundred°F (two hundred°C).

- Rub fowl breasts with olive oil, garlic powder, salt, and pepper. Place in a baking dish.
- Toss Brussels sprouts with olive oil, salt, and pepper. Spread across the hen within the baking dish.
- Bake for 25-half-hour, until bird is cooked via and Brussels sprouts are caramelized.

Timing: 35 minutes
Tips: Use a meat thermometer to ensure bird is cooked to a safe inner temperature of a hundred sixty five°F (seventy five°C).

Snack: Sliced Cucumber with Chili Lime Seasoning

INGREDIENTS
- 1 cucumber, sliced
- Chili lime seasoning to flavor

INSTRUCTIONS
- Sprinkle chili lime seasoning over sliced cucumber.

Timing: 2 mins
Tips: This snack is hydrating and coffee in calories, best for a clean choose-me-up.

Day 8

Breakfast: Cottage Cheese with Pineapple

INGREDIENTS
- 1 cup cottage cheese
- half cup pineapple chunks

INSTRUCTIONS
- Combine cottage cheese with pineapple chunks in a bowl.

Timing: 2 mins
Tips: Opt for low-fats cottage cheese for a lighter alternative while nonetheless presenting masses of protein.

Lunch: Beef and Broccoli Stir-Fry

INGREDIENTS
- 6 oz. Lean beef strips
- 1 cup broccoli florets
- 1 tbsp soy sauce
- 1 tbsp oyster sauce
- 1 garlic clove, minced
- 1 tsp ginger, grated

- 1 tbsp vegetable oil

INSTRUCTIONS
- Heat oil in a wok or massive skillet over excessive heat.
- Add garlic and ginger, stir-fry for 30 seconds.
- Add red meat strips, stir-fry for two-three minutes till browned.
- Add broccoli, soy sauce, and oyster sauce. Stir-fry for any other five mins until broccoli is gentle.

Timing: 15 mins
Tips: Slice the beef thinly in opposition to the grain for more smooth meat.

Dinner: Lemon Herb Roasted Chicken

INGREDIENTS
- 1 entire fowl, giblets removed
- 1 lemon, halved
- 4 garlic cloves
- Fresh herbs (rosemary, thyme)
- 2 tbsp olive oil
- Salt and pepper to flavor

INSTRUCTIONS
- Preheat oven to 375°F (190°C).
- Stuff the chook cavity with lemon halves, garlic cloves, and fresh herbs.
- Rub the outdoor of the chicken with olive oil, salt, and pepper.
- Roast inside the oven for 1-1.Five hours, until the juices run clear and a thermometer inserted into the thickest a part of the thigh reads a hundred sixty five°F (75°C).

Timing: 1.Five hours
Tips: Let the chicken relaxation for 10 minutes before carving to permit juices to redistribute.

Snack: Mixed Nuts

INGREDIENTS
- 1/4 cup almonds
- 1/four cup walnuts
- 1/four cup cashews

INSTRUCTIONS
Combine nuts in a small bowl or bag for an on-the-go snack.

Timing: 1 minute
Tips: Nuts are excessive in healthy fats and protein, making them an amazing snack for sustained power.

Day 9

Breakfast: Scrambled Eggs with Spinach and Mushrooms

INGREDIENTS
- three eggs
- 1 cup clean spinach
- half cup mushrooms, sliced
- 1 tbsp olive oil
- Salt and pepper to flavor

INSTRUCTIONS
- Heat olive oil in a skillet over medium warmth.
- Add mushrooms and sauté until browned, about 5 mins.
- Add spinach and cook dinner till wilted.
- Beat eggs and pour over the veggies. Cook, stirring till the eggs are set.
- Season with salt and pepper.

Timing: 10 mins
Tips: Add a sprinkle of cheese for extra flavor, in case your eating regimen permits.

Lunch: Tuna Salad

INGREDIENTS
- 1 can tuna, tired
- 1/4 cup mayonnaise, low-fats
- 1 celery stalk, diced
- 1/four onion, diced
- 1 tbsp mustard
- Salt and pepper to taste

INSTRUCTIONS
- In a bowl, blend tuna, mayonnaise, celery, onion, and mustard.
- Season with salt and pepper.

Timing: 5 mins
Tips: Serve on a mattress of greens or whole grain bread for a whole meal

Dinner: Pork Tenderloin with Roasted Sweet Potatoes

INGREDIENTS
- 1 beef tenderloin (approximately 1 lb)
- 2 sweet potatoes, cubed
- 2 tbsp olive oil
- 1 tsp paprika

- Salt and pepper to taste

INSTRUCTIONS
- Preheat oven to 375°F (190°C).
- Rub the beef tenderloin with half of the olive oil, paprika, salt, and pepper. Place in a roasting pan
- Toss sweet potatoes with the final olive oil, salt, and pepper. Spread across the pork inside the pan.
- Roast for 25-half-hour, till the red meat is cooked via and sweet potatoes are soft.

Timing: 40 minutes
Tips: Use a meat thermometer to ensure the red meat is cooked
to a safe inner temperature of 145°F (sixty three°C).

Day 10

Breakfast: Cottage Cheese Pancakes

INGREDIENTS
- half of cup cottage cheese
- 1/2 cup oat flour
- 2 eggs
- 1 tbsp honey
- half of tsp baking powder

INSTRUCTIONS
- Blend all components until smooth.
- Heat a non-stick skillet over medium warmth and pour batter to form small pancakes.
- Cook for approximately 2 mins in keeping with side till golden brown.

Timing: 15 mins
Tips: Serve with a dollop of Greek yogurt and clean berries for additonal protein and fiber.

Lunch: Spicy Grilled Shrimp Salad

INGREDIENTS
- 1 lb shrimp, peeled and deveined
- 1 tsp chili powder
- 1 tbsp olive oil
- 2 cups blended vegetables
- 1 avocado, sliced
- 1/4 cup cilantro, chopped
- 2 tbsp lime juice

INSTRUCTIONS
- Toss shrimp with chili powder and olive oil.
- Grill over medium heat for two-three mins according to facet.

- Toss combined greens with cilantro, lime juice, and top with grilled shrimp and avocado slices.

Timing: 20 minutes
Tips: Adjust the quantity of chili powder based for your spice desire.

Dinner: Beef Stroganoff with Mushroom Sauce

INGREDIENTS
- 1 lb lean red meat strips
- 1 cup mushrooms, sliced
- 1 onion, chopped
- 1 garlic clove, minced
- 1 cup red meat broth
- half of cup Greek yogurt
- 1 tbsp olive oil
- 1 tbsp Worcestershire sauce
- Salt and pepper to flavor

INSTRUCTIONS
- Heat olive oil in a skillet over medium warmness. Add beef and cook until browned. Remove and set aside.
- In the identical skillet, upload onion, garlic, and mushrooms. Cook until softened.
- Return pork to the skillet, add red meat broth and Worcestershire sauce. Simmer for 10 minutes.
- Stir in Greek yogurt, heat via without boiling. Season with salt and pepper.

Timing: half-hour
Tips: Serve over a small part of entire grain pasta or zucchini noodles.

Snack: Edamame Pods

INGREDIENTS
- 1 cup edamame pods, steamed
- Sea salt to taste

INSTRUCTIONS
- Steam edamame pods until warm.
- Sprinkle with sea salt.

Timing: 10 minutes
Tips: Edamame are extremely good for snacking as they're rich in protein and fiber.

Day 11

Breakfast: Smoothie Bowl with Nuts and Seeds

INGREDIENTS
- 1 banana
- half cup frozen berries
- 1 cup spinach
- half of cup almond milk
- 1 tbsp chia seeds
- 1 tbsp flaxseeds
- 1 tbsp pumpkin seeds
- 1 tbsp almonds, chopped

INSTRUCTIONS
- Blend banana, berries, spinach, and almond milk till smooth.
- Pour into a bowl and top with chia seeds, flaxseeds, pumpkin seeds, and almonds.

Timing: 10 minutes
Tips: The toppings upload texture and additional nutrients, making this a filling breakfast option.

Lunch: Lentil and Vegetable Stew

INGREDIENTS
- 1 cup lentils, rinsed
- 1 carrot, diced
- 1 potato, diced
- 1 onion, chopped
- 2 garlic cloves, minced
- 4 cups vegetable broth
- 1 tsp thyme
- Salt and pepper to taste

INSTRUCTIONS
- In a huge pot, sauté onion and garlic until translucent.
- Add carrots, potatoes, lentils, thyme, and vegetable broth.
- Bring to a boil, then simmer for 30 minutes until greens and lentils are soft.
- Season with salt and pepper.

Timing: forty five mins
Tips: This stew can be made in a big batch and enjoyed at some point of the week.

Dinner: Grilled Pork Chops with Apple Slaw

INGREDIENTS
- four pork chops

- 2 tbsp olive oil
- Salt and pepper to taste
- 1 apple, julienned
- 1/four cabbage, shredded
- 1 carrot, shredded
- 2 tbsp apple cider vinegar
- 1 tbsp honey

INSTRUCTIONS
- Preheat grill to medium-excessive. Rub pork chops with 1 tbsp olive oil, salt, and pepper. Grill for approximately 5-7 mins according to side.
- In a bowl, integrate apple, cabbage, carrot, apple cider vinegar, honey, and last olive oil.
- Serve grilled beef chops with apple slaw at the side.

Timing: 30 minutes
Tips: Ensure the pork chops are not too thick; otherwise, they may dry out on the grill.

Snack: Greek Yogurt with Cinnamon and Nutmeg

INGREDIENTS
- 1 cup Greek yogurt
- half of tsp cinnamon
- A pinch of nutmeg

INSTRUCTIONS
- Mix Greek yogurt with cinnamon and nutmeg.

Timing: 2 minutes
Tips: This snack is exceptional for a protein-wealthy deal with with a touch of sweetness.

Day 12

Breakfast: Avocado and Egg Breakfast Bowl

INGREDIENTS
- 1 avocado, halved and pitted
- 2 eggs
- half cup cooked quinoa
- 1 tomato, diced
- Salt and pepper to flavor
- 1 tbsp olive oil

INSTRUCTIONS
- Scoop out a piece of avocado to make room for the egg.
- Crack an egg into each avocado half.
- Season with salt and pepper, and bake at 425°F (220°C) for 15-20 minutes till the eggs are set.

- Serve with cooked quinoa and diced tomato, drizzled with olive oil.

Timing: 25 mins
Tips: This breakfast is not handiest nutritious but additionally visually appealing.

Lunch: Turkey and Spinach Wrap

INGREDIENTS
- 1 complete wheat wrap
- four ozsliced turkey breast
- 1 cup spinach
- 1/4 cup shredded carrot
- 2 tbsp hummus
- Salt and pepper to taste

INSTRUCTIONS
- Spread hummus on the wrap.
- Layer turkey, spinach, and shredded carrot.
- Roll up tightly, slice in half.

Timing: 10 minutes
Tips: This wrap is ideal for a fast, transportable lunch.

Dinner: Baked Tilapia with Lemon Herb Dressing

INGREDIENTS
- four tilapia fillets
- 2 lemons, juiced
- 1 tbsp olive oil
- 1 tsp dried herbs (thyme, rosemary)
- Salt and pepper to flavor

INSTRUCTIONS
- Preheat oven to 400°F (200°C).
- Place tilapia on a baking sheet. Drizzle with lemon juice, olive oil, and sprinkle with herbs, salt, and pepper.
- Bake for 10-12 mins, until fish flakes without problems with a fork.

Timing: 20 minutes
Tips: Serve with a facet of steamed veggies for an entire meal.

Snack: Raw Veggies and Ranch Dip

INGREDIENTS
- 1 cup raw veggies (carrots, celery, bell peppers)

- 1/4 cup ranch dressing, low-fat

INSTRUCTIONS
Serve uncooked vegetables with ranch dressing for dipping.

Timing: 5 mins
Tips: Pre-reduce vegetables at the begin of the week for easy snacking.

Day 13

Breakfast: Mixed Berry Oatmeal

INGREDIENTS
- half cup rolled oats
- 1 cup water or almond milk
- half cup mixed berries (fresh or frozen)
- 1 tbsp honey

INSTRUCTIONS
- Cook oats with water or almond milk in step with package deal directions.
- Top with mixed berries and drizzle with honey.

Timing: 10 mins
Tips: Cooking the berries with the oats can decorate their flavor and create a natural sweetness.

Lunch: Chickpea and Avocado Salad

INGREDIENTS
- 1 can chickpeas, rinsed and tired
- 1 avocado, diced
- half of cucumber, diced
- 1/four purple onion, finely chopped
- 1 tbsp olive oil
- 1 lime, juiced
- Salt and pepper to flavor

INSTRUCTIONS
- In a bowl, integrate chickpeas, avocado, cucumber, and red onion.
- Drizzle with olive oil and lime juice. Season with salt and pepper.
- Toss gently to mix.

Timing: 15 minutes
Tips: This salad is filling and can be made in advance of time, making it perfect for busy days.

Dinner: Lemon Garlic Roasted Chicken Thighs

INGREDIENTS
- four bird thighs, bone-in, pores and skin-on
- 4 garlic cloves, minced
- 1 lemon, juiced and zested
- 2 tbsp olive oil
- Salt and pepper to taste

INSTRUCTIONS
- Preheat oven to 375°F (one hundred ninety°C).
- In a bowl, blend garlic, lemon juice, zest, olive oil, salt, and pepper.
- Rub the mixture over bird thighs and vicinity in a baking dish.
- Roast for 35-forty minutes, till the skin is crispy and bird is cooked via.

Timing: 50 mins
Tips: The pores and skin have to be crispy and golden; broil for the previous couple of minutes if essential.

Snack: Apple Slices with Almond Butter

INGREDIENTS
- 1 apple, sliced
- 2 tbsp almond butter

INSTRUCTIONS
- Dip apple slices in almond butter.

Timing: 2 minutes
Tips: Choosing a crunchy apple like Honeycrisp or Fuji can beautify the texture evaluation with the creamy almond butter.

Day 14

Breakfast: Greek Yogurt Parfait

INGREDIENTS
- 1 cup Greek yogurt
- half cup granola
- half cup clean berries
- 1 tbsp honey

INSTRUCTIONS
- In a tumbler or bowl, layer Greek yogurt, granola, and berries.
- Drizzle with honey.

Timing: 5 minutes
Tips: For added texture, toast the granola gently before adding it to the parfait.

Lunch: Spiced Lentil Soup with Spinach

INGREDIENTS
- 1 cup lentils, rinsed
- 1 carrot, diced
- 1 onion, chopped
- 2 cups spinach, chopped
- 4 cups vegetable broth
- 1 tsp curry powder
- Salt and pepper to flavor

INSTRUCTIONS
- In a pot, sauté onions and carrots till gentle.
- Add lentils, broth, and curry powder. Bring to a boil, then simmer till lentils are smooth, about 20 minutes
- Stir in spinach until wilted. Season with salt and pepper.

Timing: 35 minutes
Tips: This soup is wealthy in fiber and protein, making it a filling and nutritious meal.

Dinner: Grilled Flank Steak with Chimichurri

INGREDIENTS
- 1 lb flank steak
- Salt and pepper to flavor
- half of cup clean parsley
- 1/4 cup olive oil
- 2 tbsp pink wine vinegar
- 1 garlic clove, minced
- half tsp red pepper flakes

INSTRUCTIONS
- Season steak with salt and pepper and grill to favored doneness, approximately five-7 mins per facet for medium-rare.
- Blend parsley, olive oil, vinegar, garlic, and purple pepper flakes to make chimichurri.
- Slice steak towards the grain and serve with chimichurri on top.

Timing: 20 minutes
Tips: Let the steak rest for at the least five minutes before slicing to keep it juicy.

Snack: Roasted Chickpeas

INGREDIENTS
- 1 can chickpeas, rinsed, drained, and dried
- 1 tbsp olive oil
- 1/2 tsp smoked paprika

- Salt to flavor

INSTRUCTIONS
- Toss chickpeas with olive oil, smoked paprika, and salt.
- Spread on a baking sheet and roast at four hundred°F (two hundred°C) for 20-25 minutes till crispy.

Timing: half-hour
Tips: Ensure chickpeas are thoroughly dried before roasting to reap maximum crispiness.

Day 15

Breakfast: Blueberry Almond Overnight Oats

INGREDIENTS
- half cup rolled oats
- 1/2 cup almond milk
- 1/4 cup blueberries
- 1 tbsp almond butter
- 1 tbsp chia seeds
- 1 tsp honey

INSTRUCTIONS
- In a mason jar, integrate oats, almond milk, chia seeds, and almond butter.
- Top with blueberries and drizzle with honey.
- Seal the jar and refrigerate overnight.

Timing: Overnight (five mins prep)
Tips: Stir well before consuming to mix all of the flavors.

Lunch: Grilled Vegetable and Hummus Pita

INGREDIENTS
- 1 entire wheat pita
- half cup hummus
- Assorted greens (bell peppers, zucchini, onion), grilled
- 1 tbsp olive oil
- Salt and pepper to taste

INSTRUCTIONS
- Brush greens with olive oil and grill till tender.
- Spread hummus internal pita, then fill with grilled greens.
- Season with salt and pepper.

Timing: 20 mins
Tips: This meal is perfect for meal prep—grill more vegetables and shop for quick assembly.

Dinner: Turkey Bolognese over Spaghetti Squash

INGREDIENTS
- 1 spaghetti squash, halved and seeds eliminated
- 1 lb floor turkey
- 1 can tomato sauce
- 1 onion, diced
- 2 garlic cloves, minced
- 1 tbsp olive oil
- Salt and pepper to flavor
- Fresh basil for garnish

INSTRUCTIONS
- Roast spaghetti squash at 400°F (2 hundred°C) for forty mins.
- While squash is roasting, warmness olive oil in a pan, add onion and garlic, and sauté until translucent.
- Add floor turkey, cook dinner till browned.
- Stir in tomato sauce, simmer for 10 minutes. Season with salt and pepper.
- Use a fork to scrape the spaghetti squash into strands, top with turkey bolognese and fresh basil.

Timing: 50 mins
Tips: Spaghetti squash is a extraordinary low-carb opportunity to traditional pasta, perfect for the Endomorph Diet.

Snack: Peanut Butter Celery Sticks

INGREDIENTS
- 3 celery sticks
- 2 tbsp herbal peanut butter

INSTRUCTIONS
- Spread peanut butter on each celery stick.

Timing: 5 mins
Tips: This classic snack isn't simplest crunchy however also provides a very good mix of fats and protein.

Day 16

Breakfast: Spinach and Mushroom Frittata

INGREDIENTS
- four eggs
- half of cup spinach, chopped
- half cup mushrooms, sliced
- 1/4 cup feta cheese, crumbled

- 1 tbsp olive oil
- Salt and pepper to flavor

INSTRUCTIONS
- Preheat oven to 375°F (190°C).
- Heat olive oil in an oven-safe skillet, sauté mushrooms till golden.
- Add spinach and cook dinner until wilted.
- Beat eggs and pour over greens. Sprinkle with feta cheese.
- Cook over medium heat for five minutes, then transfer to oven and bake for 15 minutes till set.

Timing: 25 mins
Tips: Frittatas are incredible for the usage of up any leftover greens you have in your refrigerator.

Lunch: Asian Chicken Salad

INGREDIENTS
- 1 chicken breast, grilled and sliced
- 2 cups combined veggies
- half cup shredded carrots
- 1/4 cup sliced almonds
- 1/4 cup mandarin oranges
- 2 tbsp sesame dressing

INSTRUCTIONS
- In a huge bowl, integrate mixed veggies, carrots, almonds, and mandarin oranges.
- Top with sliced grilled fowl.
- Drizzle with sesame dressing.

Timing: 15 minutes
Tips: This salad is a colourful and flavorful way to include a whole lot of vitamins to your weight loss plan.

Dinner: Grilled Lamb Chops with Mint Yogurt Sauce

INGREDIENTS
- 4 lamb chops
- 1 cup Greek yogurt
- 1/four cup mint leaves, finely chopped
- 2 tbsp lemon juice
- 1 garlic clove, minced
- Salt and pepper to flavor
- 1 tbsp olive oil

INSTRUCTIONS
- Season lamb chops with salt, pepper, and olive oil. Grill over medium-excessive warmness for approximately 4-five mins consistent with facet.

- In a small bowl, mix Greek yogurt, mint, lemon juice, and garlic.
- Serve lamb chops with mint yogurt sauce.

Timing: 20 mins
Tips: The mint yogurt sauce adds a sparkling, tangy evaluation to the rich taste of lamb.

Snack: Mixed Berry and Nut Mix

INGREDIENTS
- 1/4 cup uncooked almonds
- 1/four cup walnuts
- half cup dried blended berries (cranberries, blueberries, cherries)

INSTRUCTIONS
Combine almonds, walnuts, and dried berries in a small bowl or bag.

Timing: 2 mins
Tips: This snack mix is easy to carry and offers an excellent stability of nutrients.

Day 17

Breakfast: Coconut Yogurt with Flaxseeds and Mango

INGREDIENTS
- 1 cup coconut yogurt
- 1 tbsp flaxseeds
- half mango, diced

INSTRUCTIONS
- In a bowl, combine coconut yogurt with flaxseeds and pinnacle with diced mango.

Timing: five mins
Tips: Coconut yogurt is a top notch dairy-loose alternative, rich in probiotics and taste.

Lunch: Roasted Chickpea Gyros

INGREDIENTS
- 1 cup chickpeas, rinsed and tired
- 1 tbsp olive oil
- 1 tsp paprika
- 1 complete wheat pita bread
- 1/four cup tzatziki sauce
- 1/4 cucumber, sliced

- 1/4 onion, sliced

INSTRUCTIONS
- Toss chickpeas with olive oil and paprika, roast at four hundred°F (200°C) for 20 mins till crispy.
- Fill pita with roasted chickpeas, tzatziki sauce, cucumber, and onion.

Timing: 25 minutes
Tips: Roasting chickpeas adds a satisfying crunch and boosts their taste.

Dinner: Seared Scallops with Cauliflower Puree

INGREDIENTS
- 1 lb scallops
- 1 head cauliflower, chopped
- 1/four cup milk
- 2 tbsp butter
- Salt and pepper to flavor
- 1 tbsp olive oil

INSTRUCTIONS
- Boil cauliflower till very tender, drain.
- Blend cauliflower with milk, butter, salt, and pepper until easy.
- Heat olive oil in a pan, sear scallops for approximately 2 mins in line with aspect till golden.
- Serve scallops over cauliflower puree.

Timing: 30 minutes
Tips: Ensure scallops are dry before searing to get a terrific crust.

Snack: Avocado and Tomato Salad

INGREDIENTS
- 1 avocado, diced
- 1 tomato, diced
- 1 tbsp olive oil
- Salt and pepper to taste

INSTRUCTIONS
- In a bowl, combine diced avocado and tomato.
- Drizzle with olive oil, season with salt and pepper.

Timing: 5 mins
Tips: This easy salad is clean and full of healthy fat.

Day 18

Breakfast: Protein-Packed Smoothie

INGREDIENTS
- 1 scoop protein powder (chocolate or vanilla)
- 1 banana
- 1 tbsp peanut butter
- 1 cup spinach
- 1 cup almond milk

INSTRUCTIONS
- Blend all ingredients till easy.

Timing: 5 mins
Tips: This smoothie is a brief, nutritious begin to your day, perfect for mornings while you're quick on time.

Lunch: Baked Falafel Salad

INGREDIENTS
- 1 cup falafel blend (organized in keeping with bundle instructions)
- 2 cups mixed greens
- 1/four cup diced cucumber
- 1/4 cup diced tomatoes
- 1/4 cup tahini sauce

INSTRUCTIONS
- Shape falafel blend into small balls and bake at 375°F (one hundred ninety°C) for 20 minutes.
- Toss blended greens, cucumber, and tomatoes in a bowl.
- Top salad with baked falafel and drizzle with tahini sauce.

Timing: 25 mins
Tips: Baking falafel in place of frying keeps this meal mild and healthful.

Dinner: Herb-Crusted Cod with Roasted Vegetables

INGREDIENTS
- four cod fillets
- 1 tbsp combined dried herbs (thyme, rosemary, parsley)
- 2 tbsp olive oil
- 1 zucchini, sliced
- 1 bell pepper, sliced

- Salt and pepper to taste

INSTRUCTIONS
- Preheat oven to four hundred°F (200°C).
- Mix herbs with 1 tbsp olive oil, rub over cod fillets.
- Toss veggies with closing olive oil, salt, and pepper. Spread on a baking sheet.
- Place herb-crusted cod on the same baking sheet. Bake for 15-20 mins.

Timing: half-hour
Tips: This one-pan meal simplifies cleanup and packs masses of taste.

Snack: Greek Yogurt with Sunflower Seeds and Honey

INGREDIENTS
- 1 cup Greek yogurt
- 1 tbsp sunflower seeds
- 1 tbsp honey

INSTRUCTIONS
Top Greek yogurt with sunflower seeds and drizzle with honey.

Timing: 2 minutes
Tips: This snack offers an amazing balance of protein, fat, and a touch of sweetness.

Day 19

Breakfast: Poached Eggs with Avocado Toast

INGREDIENTS
- 2 eggs, poached
- 2 slices whole grain bread, toasted
- 1 avocado, mashed
- Salt and pepper to taste

INSTRUCTIONS
- Spread mashed avocado on toasted bread.
- Top each slice with a poached egg.
- Season with salt and pepper.

Timing: 10 mins
Tips: Perfecting your poached eggs will make this easy breakfast sense gourmand.

Lunch: Quinoa Tabbouleh

INGREDIENTS
- 1 cup quinoa, cooked
- 1 cup parsley, chopped

- 1/2 cup mint, chopped
- 1 tomato, diced
- 1 cucumber, diced
- 2 tbsp olive oil
- 1 lemon, juiced
- Salt and pepper to taste

INSTRUCTIONS
- In a huge bowl, combine all elements and blend well.

Timing: 15 minutes
Tips: This dish is fine served chilled, making it a first rate choice for meal prep.

Dinner: Chicken Stir-Fry with Broccoli and Bell Peppers

INGREDIENTS
- 1 lb chook breast, thinly sliced
- 1 broccoli head, reduce into florets
- 1 bell pepper, sliced
- 2 tbsp soy sauce
- 1 tbsp sesame oil
- 1 garlic clove, minced
- 1 tsp ginger, grated

INSTRUCTIONS
- Heat sesame oil in a large skillet over medium-high heat.
- Add garlic and ginger, sauté for 1 minute.
- Add bird and cook until not red.
- Add broccoli and bell pepper, cook till greens are smooth.
- Stir in soy sauce and cook dinner for some other minute.

Timing: 20 minutes
Tips: Serve over a small part of brown rice if desired, or enjoy as is for a lighter meal.

Snack: Baked Sweet Potato Chips

INGREDIENTS
- 1 sweet potato, thinly sliced
- 1 tbsp olive oil
- Salt to flavor

INSTRUCTIONS
- Toss candy potato slices with olive oil and salt.
- Spread in a single layer on a baking sheet.
- Bake at 375°F (a hundred ninety°C) for 20-25 minutes, flipping halfway thru, till crisp.

Timing: 30 minutes

Tips: Watch the chips closely to keep away from burning, as sweet potatoes can caramelize fast.

Day 20

Breakfast: Pumpkin Spice Oatmeal

INGREDIENTS
- half of cup rolled oats
- 1 cup almond milk
- 1/four cup pumpkin puree
- 1 tsp pumpkin pie spice
- 1 tbsp maple syrup
- 1 tbsp chopped pecans

INSTRUCTIONS
- In a small pot, carry almond milk to a boil.
- Add oats and reduce warmness to a simmer.
- Stir in pumpkin puree and pumpkin pie spice.
- Cook till oats are soft and creamy.
- Serve crowned with maple syrup and chopped pecans.

Timing: 10 mins
Tips: This warming breakfast is best for cooler mornings and provides a great supply of fiber.

Lunch: Grilled Chicken Caesar Wrap

INGREDIENTS
- 1 complete wheat wrap
- four ozgrilled chook breast, sliced
- 1 cup Romaine lettuce, chopped
- 2 tbsp Caesar dressing, mild
- 1/4 cup Parmesan cheese, shredded

INSTRUCTIONS
- Lay the wrap flat on a plate.
- Layer lettuce, fowl, and Parmesan cheese internal.
- Drizzle with Caesar dressing.
- Roll up the wrap tightly and slice in 1/2.

Timing: 10 minutes
Tips: Grill extra bird on the begin of the week to make meal prep faster.

Dinner: Roasted Salmon with Dill Sauce

INGREDIENTS
- 4 salmon fillets

- 2 tbsp olive oil
- Salt and pepper to flavor
- half of cup Greek yogurt
- 1 tbsp chopped clean dill
- 1 tbsp lemon juice

INSTRUCTIONS
- Preheat the oven to four hundred°F (200°C).
- Place salmon on a baking sheet, drizzle with olive oil, and season with salt and pepper.
- Roast for 12-15 mins, until cooked thru.
- Mix Greek yogurt, dill, and lemon juice in a small bowl.
- Serve salmon with a dollop of dill sauce.

Timing: 20 minutes
Tips: The dill sauce can be made earlier and stored inside the fridge for up to three days.

Snack: Cottage Cheese with Sliced Peaches

INGREDIENTS
- half cup cottage cheese
- 1 peach, sliced

INSTRUCTIONS
- Serve cottage cheese crowned with clean peach slices.

Timing: 2 minutes
Tips: Choose low-fat cottage cheese for a protein-rich snack it's decrease in calories.

Day 21

Breakfast: Egg White Scramble with Spinach and Tomatoes

INGREDIENTS
- four egg whites
- half of cup spinach, chopped
- 1/2 cup cherry tomatoes, halved
- 1 tbsp olive oil
- Salt and pepper to flavor

INSTRUCTIONS
- Heat olive oil in a skillet over medium warmness.
- Add spinach and tomatoes, prepare dinner till spinach is wilted.
- Add egg whites, scramble until cooked thru.
- Season with salt and pepper.

Timing: 10 mins

Tips: This mild breakfast is excessive in protein and low in calories, ideal for starting the day proper.

Lunch: Tuna Salad Stuffed Avocado

INGREDIENTS
- 1 can tuna, drained
- 1/four cup Greek yogurt
- 1/4 cup celery, chopped
- 1/four cup purple onion, chopped
- 2 avocados, halved and pitted
- Salt and pepper to flavor

INSTRUCTIONS
- In a bowl, blend tuna, Greek yogurt, celery, and onion.
- Season with salt and pepper.
- Scoop out some of the avocado flesh to create a larger hollow space.
- Fill avocado halves with tuna salad.

Timing: 15 minutes
Tips: This dish isn't simplest nutritious but also very filling, making it a high-quality lunch option.

Dinner: Stir-Fried Beef and Broccoli

INGREDIENTS
- 1 lb lean red meat, thinly sliced
- 2 cups broccoli florets
- 1 bell pepper, sliced
- 2 tbsp soy sauce
- 1 tbsp oyster sauce
- 1 tbsp sesame oil
- 1 garlic clove, minced

INSTRUCTIONS
- Heat sesame oil in a wok or huge skillet over high warmth.
- Add garlic and stir-fry for 30 seconds.
- Add pork and cook dinner till it starts offevolved to brown.
- Add broccoli and bell pepper, stir-fry for another 5 minutes.
- Stir in soy sauce and oyster sauce, prepare dinner for every other 2 minutes.

Timing: 20 mins
Tips: Make sure the beef is sliced thinly to ensure it chefs fast and stays gentle.

Snack: Greek Yogurt with Mixed Nuts

INGREDIENTS
- 1 cup Greek yogurt
- 1/four cup mixed nuts (almonds, walnuts, pistachios)

INSTRUCTIONS
- Top Greek yogurt with a mix of nuts.

Timing: 2 minutes
Tips: This high-protein snack will assist hold you complete and satisfied among meals.

Day 22

Breakfast: Smoothie Bowl with Kiwi and Coconut

INGREDIENTS
- 1 banana
- half of cup frozen mango
- half of cup spinach
- 1 cup coconut water
- 1 kiwi, sliced
- 1 tbsp shredded coconut

INSTRUCTIONS
- Blend banana, mango, spinach, and coconut water until clean.
- Pour right into a bowl and top with sliced kiwi and shredded coconut.

Timing: 10 minutes
Tips: This tropical smoothie bowl is not handiest scrumptious but also packed with vitamins and minerals.

Lunch: Roasted Vegetable Quinoa Salad

INGREDIENTS
- 1 cup quinoa, cooked
- 2 cups diverse veggies (zucchini, bell peppers, onions), roasted
- 1/4 cup feta cheese, crumbled
- 2 tbsp olive oil
- 1 tbsp balsamic vinegar
- Salt and pepper to flavor

INSTRUCTIONS
- In a massive bowl, blend cooked quinoa with roasted veggies.
- Add feta cheese, olive oil, and balsamic vinegar.
- Toss to mix and season with salt and pepper.

Timing: half-hour (along with roasting time)
Tips: Roast a big batch of greens at the begin of the week
to make assembling this salad short and easy.

Dinner: Lemon Herb Chicken with Asparagus

INGREDIENTS
- 4 chicken breasts
- 1 lemon, juiced and zested
- 2 tbsp clean herbs (parsley, thyme, rosemary), chopped
- 2 tbsp olive oil
- 1 lb asparagus, trimmed
- Salt and pepper to flavor

INSTRUCTIONS
- Preheat oven to 375°F (one hundred ninety°C).
- In a small bowl, mix lemon juice, zest, herbs, and olive oil.
- Place chook and asparagus in a baking dish. Pour lemon herb aggregate over the pinnacle.
- Season with salt and pepper.
- Roast for 25-30 minutes, until hen is cooked via and asparagus is gentle.

Timing: 35 minutes
Tips: Marinate the fowl inside the lemon herb mixture for
an hour before cooking for extra intense taste.

Snack: Carrot Sticks with Almond Butter

INGREDIENTS
- 1 cup carrot sticks
- 2 tbsp almond butter

INSTRUCTIONS
- Serve carrot sticks with almond butter for dipping.

Timing: 2 mins
Tips: This snack is perfect for a fast, healthy chew that provides each crunch and creaminess.

Day 23

Breakfast: Avocado and Egg Salad on Toast

INGREDIENTS
- 2 eggs, tough-boiled and chopped
- 1 avocado, mashed
- 2 slices whole grain bread, toasted
- Salt and pepper to flavor

- 1 tbsp lemon juice

INSTRUCTIONS
- In a bowl, blend chopped eggs with mashed avocado and lemon juice.
- Season with salt and pepper.
- Spread the aggregate on toasted bread slices.

Timing: 10 minutes
Tips: This breakfast isn't only filling but additionally packed with wholesome fat and proteins.

Lunch: Mediterranean Chickpea Wrap

INGREDIENTS
- 1 complete wheat wrap
- half of cup chickpeas, rinsed and drained
- 1/four cup diced cucumber
- 1/four cup diced tomatoes
- 1/four cup diced purple onion
- 1/4 cup tzatziki sauce
- 1/four cup feta cheese, crumbled

INSTRUCTIONS
- Lay the wrap flat on a plate
- Combine chickpeas, cucumber, tomatoes, and red onion in a bowl.
- Spread tzatziki sauce at the wrap, then top with the chickpea mixture and feta cheese.
- Roll up the wrap tightly and slice in 1/2.

Timing: 15 minutes
Tips: This wrap is a first rate way to comprise numerous nutrients from exceptional veggies, at the side of protein from the chickpeas.

Dinner: Grilled Tofu Steaks with Vegetable Skewers

INGREDIENTS
- 1 block firm tofu, sliced into steaks
- 1 zucchini, sliced
- 1 bell pepper, reduce into portions
- 1 onion, reduce into wedges
- 2 tbsp soy sauce
- 2 tbsp olive oil
- Salt and pepper to taste

INSTRUCTIONS
- Preheat grill to medium-high.
- Brush tofu and greens with olive oil and soy sauce. Season with salt and pepper.
- Grill tofu and vegetable skewers, turning from time to time, till charred and cooked through.

Timing: 20 mins
Tips: Pressing the tofu before marinating and grilling facilitates it absorb more taste and acquire a better texture.

Snack: Mixed Fruit Cup

INGREDIENTS
- half cup sliced strawberries
- half of cup blueberries
- half cup grapes

INSTRUCTIONS
Combine strawberries, blueberries, and grapes in a bowl.

Timing: 2 minutes
Tips: This simple fruit cup is a candy, clean snack that's also full of antioxidants.

Day 24

Breakfast: Greek Yogurt with Granola and Honey

INGREDIENTS
- 1 cup Greek yogurt
- half of cup granola
- 1 tbsp honey

INSTRUCTIONS
- In a bowl, layer Greek yogurt with granola.
- Drizzle with honey.

Timing: 2 mins
Tips: Opt for low-sugar granola to preserve this breakfast balanced and wholesome.

Lunch: Spicy Black Bean Soup

INGREDIENTS
- 1 can black beans, rinsed and tired
- 1 onion, chopped
- 2 garlic cloves, minced
- 1 bell pepper, chopped
- four cups vegetable broth
- 1 tsp cumin
- 1 tsp chili powder
- Salt and pepper to flavor

- 1 tbsp olive oil

INSTRUCTIONS
- Heat olive oil in a pot over medium warmth.
- Add onion, garlic, and bell pepper, sauté until tender.
- Add black beans, broth, cumin, and chili powder.
- Bring to a boil, then simmer for 20 mins.
- Use an immersion blender to partly combination the soup for a thicker texture.

Timing: half-hour
Tips: This hearty soup is best for a quick lunch and can be made in massive batches for meal prep.

Dinner: Herb Roasted Turkey Breast with Sweet Potatoes

INGREDIENTS
- 1 turkey breast
- 2 sweet potatoes, cubed
- 2 tbsp olive oil
- 1 tbsp combined dried herbs (rosemary, thyme, sage)
- Salt and pepper to taste

INSTRUCTIONS
- Preheat oven to 375°F (a hundred ninety°C).
- Rub turkey breast with 1 tbsp olive oil, herbs, salt, and pepper.
- Toss sweet potatoes with final olive oil and season with salt and pepper.
- Place turkey and sweet potatoes in a roasting pan.
- Roast for forty five-60 mins, until turkey is cooked via and candy potatoes are tender.

Timing: 1 hour
Tips: Use a meat thermometer to make certain the turkey is cooked to a secure inner temperature of 165°F (74°C).

Snack: Zucchini Chips

INGREDIENTS
- 1 zucchini, thinly sliced
- 1 tbsp olive oil
- Salt to taste

INSTRUCTIONS
- Toss zucchini slices with olive oil and salt.
- Spread on a baking sheet in a single layer.
- Bake at 225°F (107°C) for 1-2 hours, flipping midway via, till crisp.

Timing: 1-2 hours
Tips: Low and sluggish baking dehydrates the zucchini slices, turning them into crispy chips without frying.

Day 25

Breakfast: Pear and Walnut Oatmeal

INGREDIENTS
- half cup rolled oats
- 1 cup water or milk
- 1 pear, diced
- 1/4 cup walnuts, chopped
- 1 tsp cinnamon

INSTRUCTIONS
- Cook oats in water or milk in line with package guidelines.
- When almost accomplished, stir in diced pear and cinnamon.
- Serve topped with chopped walnuts.

Timing: 10 mins
Tips: Cooking the pear with the oatmeal will soften it and release natural sweetness.

Lunch: Spicy Lentil Wrap

INGREDIENTS
- half of cup cooked lentils
- 1 complete wheat wrap
- 1/4 cup Greek yogurt
- 1/four cup cucumber, diced
- 1/four cup tomato, diced
- 1 tsp cayenne pepper (modify to flavor)
- Salt and pepper to taste

INSTRUCTIONS
- Mix lentils with Greek yogurt, cucumber, tomato, cayenne pepper, salt, and pepper.
- Spoon the aggregate onto the wrap.
- Roll tightly and slice in half.

Timing: 10 mins
Tips: The cayenne pepper adds a spicy kick, boosting your metabolism.

Dinner: Baked Trout with Lemon and Dill

INGREDIENTS
- four trout fillets
- 2 lemons, sliced
- 4 sprigs of dill
- 2 tbsp olive oil

- Salt and pepper to taste

INSTRUCTIONS
- Preheat oven to 375°F (190°C).
- Place trout fillets on a baking sheet lined with parchment paper.
- Top every fillet with lemon slices and a sprig of dill, drizzle with olive oil.
- Season with salt and pepper.
- Bake for 15-20 mins, till the trout is flaky.

Timing: 25 mins
Tips: The lemon and dill upload a sparkling, zesty taste that complements the trout superbly.

Snack: Cucumber and Feta Cheese Bites

INGREDIENTS
- 1 cucumber, sliced into rounds
- 1/four cup feta cheese, crumbled
- 1/4 cup Greek yogurt
- Dill for garnish

INSTRUCTIONS
- Mix feta cheese with Greek yogurt.
- Top every cucumber round with a spoonful of the feta aggregate.
- Garnish with dill.

Timing: 10 mins
Tips: These bites are clean and provide an awesome blend of protein and wholesome fats.

Day 26

Breakfast: Mango Coconut Chia Pudding

INGREDIENTS
- 1/four cup chia seeds
- 1 cup coconut milk
- 1 mango, peeled and diced
- 1 tbsp honey

INSTRUCTIONS
- In a bowl, blend chia seeds with coconut milk and honey.
- Let take a seat within the refrigerator overnight.
- In the morning, top with sparkling mango.

Timing: Overnight (five minutes prep)
Tips: The mango provides herbal sweetness, whilst the chia seeds offer fiber and omega-3 fatty acids.

Lunch: Quinoa and Black Bean Salad

INGREDIENTS
- 1 cup quinoa, cooked
- half cup black beans, rinsed and tired
- half of cup corn kernels
- half of purple bell pepper, diced
- 1/4 cup cilantro, chopped
- 2 tbsp lime juice
- 1 tbsp olive oil
- Salt and pepper to flavor

INSTRUCTIONS
- In a massive bowl, combine all components.
- Toss nicely to mix. Season with salt and pepper.

Timing: 15 mins
Tips: This salad is versatile and may be served cold or at room temperature, making it ideal for meal prep.

Dinner: Herb Roasted Chicken Thighs with Brussels Sprouts

INGREDIENTS
- 4 chook thighs
- 1 lb Brussels sprouts, halved
- 2 tbsp olive oil
- 1 tsp thyme
- 1 tsp rosemary
- Salt and pepper to taste

INSTRUCTIONS
- Preheat oven to 400°F (two hundred°C).
- Place bird thighs and Brussels sprouts on a baking sheet.
- Drizzle with olive oil and sprinkle with thyme, rosemary, salt, and pepper.
- Roast for 35-forty minutes, until chicken is crispy and Brussels sprouts are caramelized.

Timing: 45 minutes
Tips: Roasting the Brussels sprouts brings out a nutty flavor that pairs properly with the herbaceous chook.

Snack: Greek Yogurt with Pomegranate Seeds

INGREDIENTS
- 1 cup Greek yogurt

- half of cup pomegranate seeds

INSTRUCTIONS
Top Greek yogurt with pomegranate seeds.

Timing: 2 mins
Tips: This snack is rich in antioxidants and protein, making it each wholesome and pleasant.

Day 27

Breakfast: Savory Spinach and Tomato Omelette

INGREDIENTS
- three eggs
- half of cup spinach, chopped
- half of tomato, diced
- 1 tbsp olive oil
- Salt and pepper to flavor

INSTRUCTIONS
- Beat eggs with salt and pepper.
- Heat olive oil in a skillet over medium warmness.
- Pour in the eggs, then sprinkle with spinach and tomato.
- Cook till the eggs are set and fold the omelette in 1/2.

Timing: 10 mins
Tips: This omelette is a brief and clean manner to begin your day with a serving of veggies.

Lunch: Mediterranean Tuna Salad

INGREDIENTS
- 1 can tuna, tired
- 1/four cup diced cucumber
- 1/four cup diced tomatoes
- 1/4 cup diced crimson onion
- 1/4 cup olives, sliced
- 2 tbsp olive oil
- 1 tbsp lemon juice
- Salt and pepper to flavor

INSTRUCTIONS
- In a bowl, blend all substances together.
- Serve chilled or at room temperature.

Timing: 10 minutes
Tips: This salad is filling and flavorful, with an excellent balance of protein and healthy fat.

Dinner: Stir-Fried Tofu with Vegetables

INGREDIENTS
- 1 block firm tofu, reduce into cubes
- 1 cup broccoli florets
- 1 carrot, sliced
- 1 bell pepper, sliced
- 2 tbsp soy sauce
- 1 tbsp sesame oil
- 1 garlic clove, minced
- 1 tsp ginger, grated

INSTRUCTIONS
- Press tofu for 30 minutes to remove extra water.
- Heat sesame oil in a massive skillet or wok over medium-high heat.
- Add garlic and ginger, sauté for 1 minute.
- Add tofu and veggies, stir-fry till greens are soft and tofu is golden.
- Drizzle with soy sauce and stir to combine.

Timing: half-hour
Tips: Pressing the tofu helps it better absorb the flavors and acquire a crispy outside whilst stir-fried.

Snack: Almonds and Dried Cranberries

INGREDIENTS
- 1/four cup almonds
- 1/4 cup dried cranberries

INSTRUCTIONS
- Mix almonds and dried cranberries collectively.

Timing: 1 minute
Tips: This snack blend is straightforward to hold and presents an excellent balance of sweet and nutty flavors.

Day 28

Breakfast: Banana Nut Muffins

INGREDIENTS
- 2 bananas, mashed
- 1/4 cup honey
- 1/four cup vegetable oil
- 1 egg
- half of tsp vanilla extract
- 1 cup complete wheat flour

- half tsp baking soda
- 1/4 tsp salt
- half of cup walnuts, chopped

INSTRUCTIONS
- Preheat oven to 375°F (190°C).
- In a bowl, mix bananas, honey, oil, egg, and vanilla.
- In any other bowl, combine flour, baking soda, and salt.
- Mix dry components into wet substances till just mixed. Fold in walnuts.
- Spoon batter into muffin tins and bake for 20 minutes.

Timing: 30 minutes
Tips: These muffins are first rate for breakfast on-the-move and may be stored for several days.

Lunch: Avocado Chicken Salad

INGREDIENTS
- 1 fowl breast, cooked and shredded
- 1 avocado, mashed
- 1/4 cup Greek yogurt
- 1/4 cup celery, diced
- 1/4 cup red onion, diced
- 1 tbsp lime juice
- Salt and pepper to flavor

INSTRUCTIONS
- In a bowl, blend all substances together till well mixed.
- Season with salt and pepper.
- Serve on complete wheat bread or over a bed of greens.

Timing: 15 minutes
Tips: This salad is creamy and pleasurable, offering an awesome stability of protein and wholesome fats.

Dinner: Quinoa Stuffed Peppers

INGREDIENTS
- four bell peppers, tops cut off and seeded
- 1 cup quinoa, cooked
- 1 can black beans, rinsed and tired
- 1 cup corn kernels
- half of cup tomatoes, diced
- half of cup shredded cheddar cheese
- 1 tsp cumin

- Salt and pepper to flavor

INSTRUCTIONS
- Preheat oven to 375°F (one hundred ninety°C).
- In a bowl, blend quinoa, black beans, corn, tomatoes, cumin, salt, and pepper.
- Stuff combination into bell peppers, pinnacle with cheese.
- Place in a baking dish with a little water on the lowest. Cover with foil.
- Bake for 30-35 minutes, until peppers are tender.

Timing: 50 mins
Tips: These filled peppers are colorful and nutritious, perfect for a satisfying meal.

Snack: Greek Yogurt with Blueberries and Honey

INGREDIENTS
- 1 cup Greek yogurt
- 1/2 cup blueberries
- 1 tbsp honey

INSTRUCTIONS
- Top Greek yogurt with blueberries and drizzle with honey.

Timing: 2 mins
Tips: This snack is an remarkable supply of protein and antioxidants, making it each healthy and scrumptious.

Day 29

Breakfast: Sweet Potato Hash with Eggs

INGREDIENTS
- 1 sweet potato, peeled and diced
- half of onion, diced
- 1 bell pepper, diced
- 2 eggs
- 2 tbsp olive oil
- Salt and pepper to taste

INSTRUCTIONS
- Heat olive oil in a massive skillet over medium heat.
- Add candy potato, onion, and bell pepper. Cook till soft and slightly caramelized.
- Create wells within the hash and crack an egg into every.
- Cover and prepare dinner until eggs are set.
- Season with salt and pepper.

Timing: 25 minutes
Tips: This hearty breakfast is a flavorful way to start the day with a great mix of carbs, protein, and fats.

Lunch: Greek Salad with Grilled Chicken

INGREDIENTS
- 2 cups combined greens
- half cup cherry tomatoes, halved
- 1/4 cup cucumber, sliced
- 1/4 cup crimson onion, thinly sliced
- 1/4 cup Kalamata olives, pitted
- 1/four cup feta cheese, crumbled
- four ozgrilled bird breast, sliced
- 2 tbsp olive oil
- 1 tbsp pink wine vinegar
- Salt and pepper to flavor

INSTRUCTIONS
- In a huge bowl, integrate vegetables, tomatoes, cucumber, onion, olives, and feta cheese.
- Top with sliced grilled chicken.
- Drizzle with olive oil and purple wine vinegar. Season with salt and pepper.

Timing: 15 mins
Tips: This salad is a clean and protein-wealthy lunch option, ideal for a light yet satisfying meal.

Dinner: Baked Cod with a Herb Crust

INGREDIENTS
- four cod fillets
- 1/4 cup breadcrumbs
- 1/4 cup Parmesan cheese, grated
- 2 tbsp clean parsley, chopped
- 2 tbsp olive oil
- Salt and pepper to taste

INSTRUCTIONS
- Preheat oven to four hundred°F (200°C).
- Mix breadcrumbs, Parmesan, parsley, and olive oil in a bowl.
- Season cod with salt and pepper, then pinnacle each fillet with the breadcrumb combination.
- Bake for 15-20 mins, till the crust is golden and cod is cooked via.

Timing: 25 minutes
Tips: This dish offers a satisfying crunch and taste enhance to the slight cod.

Snack: Apple Slices with Almond Butter

INGREDIENTS
- 1 apple, sliced

- 2 tbsp almond butter

INSTRUCTIONS
- Serve apple slices with almond butter for dipping.

Timing: 2 mins
Tips: This snack is a perfect combo of sweet and creamy flavors, providing both fiber and healthy fat.

Day 30

Breakfast: Avocado Smoothie

INGREDIENTS
- 1 ripe avocado
- 1 banana
- 1 cup spinach
- 1 cup almond milk
- 1 tbsp honey

INSTRUCTIONS
- Blend all components until easy.

Timing: five minutes
Tips: This smoothie is thick, creamy, and packed with vitamins, making it a extraordinary start to your day.

Lunch: Veggie Hummus Sandwich

INGREDIENTS
- 2 slices complete grain bread
- 1/4 cup hummus
- 1/4 avocado, sliced
- 1/four cucumber, sliced
- 1/4 pink bell pepper, sliced
- 1/4 cup alfalfa sprouts

INSTRUCTIONS
- Spread hummus on both slices of bread.
- Layer avocado, cucumber, bell pepper, and sprouts on one slice.
- Top with the alternative slice and press lightly.

Timing: 10 mins
Tips: This sandwich is bursting with flavor and texture, plus it's packed with fiber.

Dinner: Thai Coconut Curry with Shrimp

INGREDIENTS
- 1 lb shrimp, peeled and deveined
- 1 can coconut milk
- 1 tbsp Thai curry paste
- half bell pepper, sliced
- half of onion, sliced
- 1 carrot, julienned
- 1 tbsp fish sauce
- 1 tsp sugar
- half lime, juiced
- Cilantro for garnish

INSTRUCTIONS
- In a big skillet, heat coconut milk and curry paste over medium heat.
- Add onion, bell pepper, and carrot. Cook until greens are gentle.
- Add shrimp and prepare dinner until pink and opaque.
- Stir in fish sauce, sugar, and lime juice.
- Garnish with cilantro earlier than serving.

Timing: half-hour
Tips: Serve this fragrant curry over a small serving of rice or on my own for a decrease-carb alternative.

Snack: Baked Pear with Cinnamon and Walnuts

INGREDIENTS
- 1 pear, halved and cored
- 1/4 cup walnuts, chopped
- 1 tsp cinnamon
- 1 tbsp honey

INSTRUCTIONS
- Preheat oven to 350°F (a hundred seventy five°C).
- Place pear halves on a baking sheet, sprinkle with cinnamon and walnuts, and drizzle with honey.
- Bake for 20-25 mins, until pears are soft.

Timing: half-hour
Tips: This warm, comforting snack is perfect for ending the day on a candy be aware.

Part IV
CUSTOMIZING THE EXERCISE REGIMEN

Chapter 5
TRAINING PRINCIPLES SPECIFIC TO ENDOMORPHS

Endomorphs, one of the 3 number one frame types alongside ectomorphs and mesomorphs, have a tendency to have a clearly better frame fats percent, a extensive bone structure, and may benefit muscle and fat pretty without problems. Developing an effective training approach for endomorphs requires an know-how in their specific physiological developments. These people often struggle with weight management, but with the right technique, they could achieve top notch health outcomes. This chapter delves into the position of High-Intensity Interval Training (HIIT) and strength schooling, highlighting their importance in fats loss and muscle building for endomorphs.

Endomorphs are often characterised with the aid of a propensity to save fat, which may be a double-edged sword. On one hand, it lets in them to have enough power reserves, however on the alternative, it predisposes them to weight benefit, particularly if their life-style is sedentary. This herbal inclination underscores the necessity of incorporating rigorous and centered bodily sports that cater mainly to their frame type.

High-Intensity Interval Training (HIIT) for Endomorphs

HIIT involves brief bursts of intense exercise alternated with low-intensity recovery intervals. Interestingly, it is a time-efficient way to exercising and has been proven to provide advanced fats-burning advantages in comparison to constant-state aerobic. For endomorphs, HIIT is especially wonderful because it addresses their want to lose fat without the time commitment required by means of different types of exercise.

One of the primary blessings of HIIT for endomorphs is its potential to increase the resting metabolic charge for hours after workout, a phenomenon referred to as excess publish-exercising oxygen intake (EPOC). This means that even after the schooling consultation has ended, the body keeps to burn calories at a higher price. For endomorphs, who certainly have a slower metabolism, this may extensively aid in weight control and fats loss.

Moreover, HIIT allows to improve insulin sensitivity, a not unusual issue among endomorphs. Improved insulin sensitivity way the frame can use glucose greater effectively, decreasing the likelihood of sugar being stored as fat. This is especially critical for endomorphs, as they may be more susceptible to insulin resistance, that could lead to kind 2 diabetes and other metabolic troubles.

Incorporating HIIT into an endomorph's ordinary may be achieved in numerous ways, which includes sprinting, cycling, bounce rope, or maybe through circuit education that consists of excessive-intensity physical activities with minimum relaxation among sets.

The secret is to push the body to its restriction during the extreme levels and permit good enough healing at some stage in the low-depth intervals. Strength education is an necessary component of any health routine, especially for endomorphs, who generally tend to have a certainly better frame fats percentage and a slower metabolism. The aim of electricity schooling goes past simply growing muscle groups; it additionally entails improving metabolic price and enhancing ordinary frame composition, that are essential for powerful weight control and fitness improvement.

The Importance of Muscle Mass

For endomorphs, muscular tissues is not just a issue in bodily electricity and appearance; it also performs a important function in metabolic health. Muscle tissue is metabolically active, that means it burns energy even when at relaxation. This feature is especially beneficial for endomorphs, because it helps offset their naturally lower basal metabolic charge. By incorporating everyday strength education into their health routines, endomorphs can increase their resting metabolic fee (RMR), which enhances their capability to burn energy in the course of the day and assists in long-time period fat loss and weight management.

Optimal Strength Training Practices

Strength education for endomorphs must be based to maximise fats loss while promoting muscle increase. This may be completed thru a mixture of weightlifting and bodyweight physical games. Focusing on compound moves is mainly powerful; sporting activities like squats, deadlifts, and bench presses engage more than one big muscle organizations simultaneously, worrying greater power and yielding better calorie-burning and muscle-building outcomes. These sporting events are foundational because they replicate useful actions utilized in each day sports, which allows in reducing the danger of injuries with the aid of strengthening the muscle tissues and joints needed for not unusual obligations. Moreover, compound moves stimulate the production of anabolic hormones, which are crucial for muscle growth and restoration.

High-Intensity Strength Training

To further beautify the effectiveness of electricity schooling, endomorphs can rent high-intensity techniques. One such approach is the usage of supersets, which entails acting two sporting events back-to-returned with out a relaxation in among. This approach now not only saves time but additionally will increase the intensity of the exercise, main to better calorie burn and a more potent stimulus for muscle growth. For instance, pairing a lower frame exercising like squats with an higher body workout including bench presses can keep the heart price elevated and ensure that different muscle corporations are being labored continuously.

Another effective technique is pyramid schooling, in which the burden is improved or reduced with every set, and the repetitions are adjusted as a consequence. This technique enables in regularly warming up the muscle mass with lighter weights and better reps, after which growing the depth with heavier weights and fewer reps, which is first-rate for constructing electricity and muscle mass.

Integrating Strength Training with HIIT

Combining power education with High-Intensity Interval Training (HIIT) may be mainly beneficial for endomorphs. Starting a exercising consultation with a HIIT routine can elevate the heart rate and kickstart the fats-burning manner. Following up with a electricity training phase allows the body to hold burning fat even as additionally focusing on muscle constructing. This method ensures a comprehensive exercising that addresses both principal concerns of endomorphs: fats loss and muscle benefit. For instance, a normal combined session might begin with 15-20 mins of HIIT, which includes cycles of sprinting and strolling or other high-depth activities. This might be observed through a electricity schooling routine focusing on compound movements, supplemented by way of high-depth strategies like supersets or pyramid sets. Such a regimen now not handiest maximizes metabolic blessings however also maintains the workout routines various and challenging, assisting to keep motivation and consistency.

Practical Considerations and Adjustments

When embarking on a power training program, it is critical for endomorphs to recollect their individual reaction to workout. Monitoring progress and making changes based on effects is prime to finding the handiest regimen. Additionally, right nutrients performs an essential role in assisting muscle increase and restoration. A weight-reduction plan wealthy in proteins, balanced with wholesome fats and carbohydrates, and good enough hydration are essential for powerful restoration and muscle synthesis. Strength schooling gives a robust street for endomorphs to enhance their metabolism, boom muscle groups, and enhance normal frame composition. By focusing on compound actions, incorporating excessive-depth schooling strategies, and integrating strength classes with HIIT, endomorphs can create a powerful, fats-burning, muscle-building application tailored to their specific physiological needs. This complete approach no longer most effective aids in weight control however additionally contributes to universal fitness and well-being, paving the manner for a more healthy life-style.

Practical Considerations for Endomorph Training

When designing a training software for endomorphs, it is vital to take into account frequency and consistency. Regularity in training periods, ideally four to five times a week, is crucial for maintaining progress and accomplishing vast results. Additionally, each consultation have to include a mixture of HIIT and power schooling to maximize fats loss and muscle increase.

Diet also plays a crucial position inside the effectiveness of any schooling application for endomorphs. A well-balanced eating regimen that makes a speciality of entire ingredients and avoids excess carbohydrates and fat is essential. Combining a solid weight loss plan with an powerful schooling software is the high-quality manner to make sure success for endomorphs.

Understanding the precise needs and demanding situations of the endomorph frame type is vital in crafting an effective health program. By incorporating HIIT for efficient fats burning and electricity education for muscle building, endomorphs can create a balanced technique to fitness that ends in sustainable weight control and improved health. With the proper education principles and determination, endomorphs can conquer their natural predispositions and achieve their health dreams.

Part V
MAINTAINING MOTIVATION AND OVERCOMING CHALLENGES

Chapter 6
MONITORING YOUR PROGRESS

Achieving health and fitness desires is a journey that requires endurance, dedication, and a strategic method. Monitoring progress is vital, as it allows individuals to stay stimulated, adjust techniques, and acquire success in a dependent way. This chapter delves into the significance of placing practical goals and milestones, in addition to adapting your plan to satisfy evolving wishes during your health journey.

The Importance of Setting Realistic Goals

Embarking on a fitness journey is an thrilling enterprise, however without clean, potential, and meaningful dreams, it is able to fast end up aimless and demotivating. The basis of any successful fitness routine hinges on putting sensible desires that now not simplest stretch your skills but additionally take into account your present day physical condition, lifestyle constraints, and long-time period aspirations. Whether your purpose is to shed pounds, construct muscle, enhance cardiovascular fitness, or definitely boom day by day pastime, the established order of nicely-defined desires is crucial.

Understanding Realistic Goal Setting

Realistic desires are those which can be manageable within a particular time-frame and don't forget private boundaries and assets. Setting an impossible purpose, together with losing 50 pounds in a month, can cause frustration and capability fitness risks. Conversely, a realistic and healthful purpose might be aiming to lose 1-2 kilos per week, placing the degree for sustainable, lengthy-time period weight loss.

The method of placing those dreams starts offevolved with a complete assessment of your bodily condition, that is ideally carried out below the steerage of a healthcare provider or a fitness expert. This evaluation can also include evaluating your frame mass index (BMI), frame fats percentage, muscle tissues, and other critical health signs like blood stress and cholesterol levels. Such metrics offer a baseline from which development can be measured and are essential for tailoring a health software that addresses your particular wishes.

Short-time period and Long-time period Goal Planning

Once you've got installed a clean know-how of your contemporary health reputation, the subsequent step is to set both short-term and long-time period goals. Short-term goals are instantaneous targets that function stepping stones towards your remaining targets. They are designed to be achievable inside a shorter time frame and aim to preserve you engaged and committed to the technique. For example, if your long-term purpose is to run a marathon, a appropriate quick-time period intention may be to run a positive distance each week or month, progressively increasing your stamina and endurance.

Long-term desires, then again, are more formidable and require a sustained attempt over the years. These are the large-photograph dreams that would appear daunting in the beginning however are attainable with persistence and willpower. They need to be simply aligned together with your remaining aspirations and mirror what you hope to accomplish through your health journey.

The Role of Milestones

Milestones are precise markers set along the course for your long-time period goals. Unlike fashionable short-term desires, milestones are in particular widespread achievements that demonstrate clean development towards your closing goal. For instance, a milestone in a weight reduction adventure may be fitting into a selected piece of apparel or accomplishing a selected weight elegance. In training contexts, it is able to be accomplishing a brand new non-public excellent in a 5K run or correctly completing a challenging health magnificence with out breaks. Setting milestones is important as it breaks the long-time period intention into possible chunks, making the procedure less overwhelming and more based. Each milestone completed is a testomony to your effort and endurance, which is distinctly motivating.

Celebrating Milestones

The significance of celebrating milestones can not be overstated. Recognition of your achievements, no matter how small, performs a vital position in maintaining motivation and exuberance. Celebrations can be as simple as taking a time off to relax, shopping for new exercise equipment, or enjoying a small deal with. The act of celebrating no longer best rewards your hard paintings but additionally reinforces the fine behavior had to maintain pursuing further goals.

Setting Goals in a Real-World Context

To make goal-placing even more effective, they should be SMART: Specific, Measurable, Achievable, Relevant, and Time-sure. This criterion ensures that goals are properly-described and inside reach. For instance, in place of putting a indistinct intention like "get match," a SMART goal might be "to lose 10 pounds in ninety days with the aid of workout for half-hour a day, five days a week and consuming a balanced food regimen of 1800 energy each day." This aim isn't always most effective unique and measurable however additionally includes a time-frame and details about how the goal can be finished.

Setting sensible desires is the cornerstone of any a success fitness journey. By organising clean, doable goals, developing based milestones, and celebrating achievements, people can hold motivation and enjoy a experience of feat throughout their progress. Moreover, adapting goals to align with private increase and changing circumstances ensures that the health adventure stays applicable and targeted, main to sustained achievement and well-being.

Adapting the Plan to Evolving Needs

As you progress for your health adventure, your wishes and competencies will unavoidably alternate. The health plan you to start with start with may not remain powerful or applicable as you increase, necessitating modifications to accommodate new dreams, advanced talents, or modified circumstances. Adapting your health plan is essential to maintaining progress, stopping plateaus, decreasing the threat of injuries, and maintaining hobby and motivation through the years. Understanding how to effectively adapt your fitness routine could make the difference among a stagnant or thriving course to health and well-being.

Regular Assessments of Physical Condition

One of the cornerstones of adapting your health plan successfully is the normal re-assessment of your physical condition. This ongoing evaluation process includes greater than just stepping on a scale; it features a comprehensive analysis of frame composition, fitness levels, and ordinary fitness indicators. For instance, after numerous months of schooling, a re-evaluation of your frame composition can provide insights into modifications in muscle groups, fats percent, and other critical metrics. These records factors are crucial for informing the necessary modifications in your fitness regimen.

Periodic tests also can amplify to revisiting nutritional wishes with a nutritionist. Nutritional requirements can shift significantly based totally on adjustments to your workout intensity, muscle mass, or even preferences. For instance, increasing muscle tissue now not handiest adjustments how your frame seems however additionally enhances your metabolic price, which could boom your caloric desires. If those new desires aren't met, your development can stall, and you might even revel in fatigue and different fitness issues. Similarly, enhancements in your cardiovascular and muscular staying power can also let you engage in more excessive or extended workout routines, necessitating modifications in both your workout and vitamins plans.

Flexibility in Setting and Adjusting Goals

Flexibility is an critical factor of any long-time period health strategy. Your adventure is probably to encounter diverse limitations and opportunities, together with life occasions, changes in bodily or mental fitness, or shifts in interests and priorities. Being bendy for your approach allows you to regulate your desires with out feeling as even though you've got failed when faced with unexpected demanding situations or whilst seizing new possibilities.

For example, sustaining a minor harm could derail plans for jogging a marathon, but adjusting your goal to increase day by day steps or to perform low-effect physical games can keep you energetic and save you feelings of frustration and stagnation. Similarly, coming across a ardour for a brand new type of workout, together with cycling, yoga, or swimming, would possibly lead you to combine these sports into your routine, which could renew your enthusiasm and probably accelerate your development towards broader health desires.

Continuous Learning and Education

The fields of fitness, vitamins, and physical health are constantly evolving, with new studies findings often tough old paradigms. Staying knowledgeable approximately the latest studies and developments is vital for the continued edition of your health plan. This continuous mastering process allow you to incorporate new, greater effective physical games, discard old practices, and optimize your diet primarily based at the ultra-modern dietary technological know-how.

For instance, new studies into c program languageperiod schooling may monitor greater efficient approaches to burn fat, or rising statistics approximately plant-based totally diets should provide insights into reducing irritation and enhancing recuperation. By staying knowledgeable and educated, you can make well-based choices that preserve your health adventure aligned with the first-rate to be had evidence, making sure that your body is receiving the most effective care and training.

Implementing Technology and Tools

In modern virtual age, diverse technological gear can help in monitoring and adapting your fitness plan. Fitness trackers, smartwatches, and cellular apps provide actual-time records to your bodily sports, sleep styles, heart rate, and extra, providing insights which could help best-tune your exercise and dietary desires. Additionally, online systems and apps can provide personalised training regimens and dietary hints that adapt dynamically as your health stages change.

These tools can be in particular beneficial for placing particular, measurable goals and for tracking progress in actual-time, presenting a motivational enhance and assisting you stay devoted in your adjusted plan. For instance, seeing the variety of steps growth, calories burned, or heart charge lower all through exercises can offer immediate comments that your efforts are yielding results.

Adapting to Psychological and Emotional Changes

Finally, it's critical to apprehend and adapt to mental and emotional modifications at some point of your health adventure. Your intellectual fitness affects your bodily fitness, and vice versa. Activities together with meditation, yoga, or even speaking cures can be incorporated into your fitness routine to help manipulate pressure, enhance mental resilience, and preserve motivation.

As you still adapt your plan, normal mirrored image on your achievements, challenges, and the joy you derive from your fitness recurring can hold you grounded and focused. Acknowledging the mental and emotional components of your health journey ensures a holistic approach to fitness that aligns your bodily activities with your general well-being. Adapting your health plan as you development isn't just about changing workout routines or food plan however involves a complete, responsive technique that considers modifications in physical condition, personal alternatives, life-style adjustments, and mental nicely-being. By embracing flexibility, non-stop gaining knowledge of, and the combination of era, you could make certain that your health adventure stays dynamic, effective, and aligned together with your evolving desires. This adaptive method not handiest optimizes physical fitness outcomes however also complements the general exceptional of existence, making the pursuit of fitness and health a always worthwhile enjoy.

Chapter 7
SUCCESS STORIES

Success stories aren't simply stories of success; they are narratives of transformation, resilience, and the triumph of the human spirit. In the context of the Endomorph Diet and Exercise Plan, achievement tales function effective motivators, demonstrating that with willpower, perseverance, and the proper techniques, anybody can gain their fitness and health goals. This bankruptcy stocks inspiring tales of individuals who have converted their lives through the Endomorph Diet and Exercise Plan, showcasing the tangible effects that may be performed with commitment and determination.

Sarah's Journey to Health and Happiness

Sarah's tale is a testament to the transformative electricity of the Endomorph Diet and Exercise Plan. At the start of her journey, Sarah was overweight, torpid, and suffering with low self-esteem. She had tried severa diets and exercise regimens inside the beyond but had constantly struggled to keep them lengthy-time period. Determined to make a long-lasting trade, Sarah embraced the Endomorph Diet and Exercise Plan with gusto. She started out by placing practical dreams, focusing on sluggish weight reduction and progressed fitness as opposed to quick fixes. Sarah included a whole lot of physical games into her routine, consisting of HIIT workouts, power education, and flexibility exercises, to keep her workouts interesting and hard.

Sarah additionally paid close attention to her food plan, following the Endomorph Diet recommendations to ensure she turned into consuming the proper foods within the proper quantities. She discovered to listen to her body's hunger cues and made conscious selections to fuel her body with nutritious ingredients that supported her dreams. Over time, Sarah started out to see significant adjustments in her frame and common properly-being. She lost weight, gained muscle tone, and felt more energized than ever earlier than. But possibly most significantly, Sarah's confidence soared. She no longer felt self-aware of her appearance however as a substitute embraced her newfound strength and power.

Today, Sarah is a true fulfillment story. She has maintained her weight reduction, continued to prioritize her fitness and fitness, and evokes others together with her adventure. Sarah's tale serves as a reminder that with dedication, perseverance, and the proper attitude, whatever is feasible.

John's Transformation from Couch Potato to Fitness Enthusiast

John's tale is one in every of radical transformation. Just a few years ago, John became a self-professed couch potato. He led a sedentary lifestyle, indulging in unhealthy ingredients and infrequently engaging in bodily interest. As a end result, John was obese, not worthy, and unhappy with his appearance and fitness. Determined to show his life round, John decided to commit to the Endomorph Diet and Exercise Plan. He commenced via gradually incorporating extra motion into his day, beginning with short walks and regularly increasing the intensity and length of his workout routines. John additionally overhauled his eating regimen, slicing out processed meals, sugar, and dangerous fat, and as a substitute specializing in whole, nutrient-dense meals. He discovered to cook healthful meals at home and have become extra conscious of his component sizes and eating behavior. As John's health level improved, he started to mission himself with extra excessive workouts, together with weightlifting and aerobic periods. He additionally joined a neighborhood health institution, which furnished him with aid and motivation on his adventure.

Today, John is unrecognizable from his former self. He has misplaced a sizeable quantity of weight, received muscular tissues, and improved his typical health and health levels. But perhaps most importantly, John has determined a newfound ardour for fitness and a zest for lifestyles that he in no way knew existed.John's story is a reminder that it is never too overdue to make a alternate. With willpower, commitment, and the right help, each person can rework their lifestyles and attain their health and health desires.

Emily's Journey to Self-Acceptance and Empowerment

Emily's tale is a poignant reminder that fitness and health aren't pretty much physical look however also about intellectual and emotional well-being. For years, Emily struggled with frame photograph issues, constantly comparing herself to others and feeling insecure about her appearance. Determined to break loose from this cycle of negativity, Emily embarked on a adventure of self-discovery and empowerment through the Endomorph Diet and Exercise Plan. She commenced by means of reframing her mind-set, specializing in self-love and acceptance in place of complaint and judgment. Emily also embraced a holistic method to health, prioritizing no longer simply her physical fitness but also her mental and emotional nicely-being. She practiced mindfulness and meditation, engaged in sports that brought her joy, and surrounded herself with wonderful impacts.

As Emily's self-esteem grew, so too did her commitment to her fitness and health desires. She observed pleasure in movement, discovering a love for yoga, dance, and other kinds of exercising that nourished her frame and soul. She additionally embraced the Endomorph Diet concepts, choosing ingredients that made her feel suitable from the interior out. Today, Emily radiates confidence and self-guarantee. She has embraced her frame and celebrates its electricity and resilience. Emily's journey is a reminder that actual health and health come from within and that self-love and attractiveness are crucial components of any a success fitness adventure.

These fulfillment tales are only a few examples of the endless individuals who have converted their lives through the Endomorph Diet and Exercise Plan. They serve as effective reminders that with willpower, perseverance, and the right mind-set, whatever is viable. Whether you're trying to lose weight, build muscle, or without a doubt improve your overall health and properly-being, the Endomorph Diet and Exercise Plan will let you attain your goals. So, what are you expecting? Start your journey nowadays and be a part of the ranks of those inspiring achievement memories!

Bonus Chapter
BUILDING YOUR TRAINING PLAN

Creating an effective schooling plan is vital for achieving your health desires, whether you are aiming to shed pounds, build muscle, or enhance your general health and health. This chapter presents a complete guide to constructing a education plan that is tailored on your wishes and desires. We'll explore the important thing components of a a success training program, which include placing desires, selecting the proper sporting activities, and designing a workout schedule that works for you.

Setting Your Goals

The first step in building your training plan is to define your goals. What do you need to obtain along with your health software? Are you looking to shed pounds, build muscle, improve your cardiovascular fitness, or all of the above? Setting clear, workable desires will assist you live encouraged and targeted for the duration of your training. When placing your goals, it is critical to be precise and sensible. Instead of putting a vague intention like "get in shape," attempt placing a specific intention like "lose 10 pounds in 3 months" or "growth my bench press by using 20 kilos." This will give you a clean target to aim for and could help you song your progress alongside the way.

Selecting the Right Exercises

Once you've got defined your desires, the following step is to pick the right exercises that will help you achieve them. The key's to pick out physical games that target more than one muscle agencies and are suitable on your fitness level. For instance, compound physical games like squats, deadlifts, and bench presses are high-quality for constructing electricity and muscle groups, at the same time as cardio physical activities like strolling, cycling, and swimming are effective for enhancing cardiovascular fitness. It's also critical to differ your sporting activities to save you boredom and plateaus. Incorporating a mixture of electricity education, cardio, and flexibility sporting activities into your habitual will help hold things exciting and make sure that you're working all components of your fitness.

Designing Your Workout Schedule

With your desires and exercises decided on, the next step is to layout your exercise schedule. This will depend on elements like your fitness stage, agenda, and goals, but a general guideline is to aim for at the least 3 days of exercising according to week, with a mix of strength education and aerobic.

When designing your agenda, it is vital to encompass rest days to allow your muscle tissues time to recover and repair. Overtraining can cause damage and burnout, so concentrate for your body and provide your self permission to take a day without work when wished.

Sample Training Program for Men and Women

To come up with an idea of what a education program would possibly appear to be, here is a sample software for both males and females:

Sample Training Program for Men

Day 1 - Upper Body Strength

- Bench Press: 3 units of 8-12 reps
- Pull-Ups: three sets of eight-12 reps
- Shoulder Press: 3 units of eight-12 reps
- Bicep Curls: three sets of eight-12 reps
- Tricep Dips: 3 units of 8-12 reps

Day 2 - Lower Body Strength

- Squats: three units of eight-12 reps
- Deadlifts: three units of 8-12 reps
- Lunges: 3 sets of eight-12 reps per leg
- Calf Raises: 3 units of eight-12 reps

Day 3 - Cardio

- 30 minutes of mild-intensity cardio (e.G., walking, cycling, swimming)
- Day four - Rest
- Day five - Upper Body Strength

Day 4 - Lower Body Strength

- Same as Day 2

Day 7 - Rest

Sample Training Program for Women

Day 1

- Full Body Strength
- Squats: three units of 8-12 reps
- Deadlifts: three units of eight-12 reps
- Bench Press: 3 units of eight-12 reps
- Pull-Ups (assisted if wanted): three units of eight-12 reps
- Shoulder Press: 3 sets of eight-12 reps
- Plank: 3 units of 30-60 seconds

Day 2 - Cardio

- half-hour of mild-depth aerobic
- Day three - Rest

Day3 - Lower Body Strength

- Lunges: three sets of eight-12 reps per leg
- Calf Raises: three units of eight-12 reps
- Leg Press: three units of 8-12 reps
- Glute Bridges: 3 sets of eight-12 reps
- Day five - Upper Body Strength

Same as Day 1

Day 6 - Cardio

half-hour of mild-intensity cardio

Day 7 - Rest

Building an powerful education plan requires careful attention of your goals, health degree, and schedule. By putting clear dreams, selecting the right sporting activities, and designing a exercising time table that works for you, you may create a schooling software that will help you gain your health goals and enhance your overall health and well-being. Remember to concentrate on your frame, stay steady, and adjust your plan as needed to make certain persisted development and success.

CONCLUSION

In conclusion, constructing a training plan that fits your dreams, way of life, and fitness degree is vital for accomplishing fulfillment on your fitness and fitness journey. Here are the key factors to recall:

- Set Clear, Achievable Goals: Define what you need to attain and break it down into smaller, possible desires.
- Choose the Right Exercises: Select physical activities that target multiple muscle agencies and are appropriate on your health stage.
- Design a Balanced Workout Schedule: Include a mixture of energy schooling, cardio, and versatility physical activities, and consider to consist of relaxation days.
- Listen to Your Body: Pay interest to how your frame responds to workout and regulate your plan therefore.
- Stay Consistent: Consistency is key to seeing consequences, so persist with your plan even when it receives hard.
- Be Flexible: Life may be unpredictable, so be willing to evolve your plan when wished.
- Seek Support: Whether it is from a chum, a private instructor, or an internet network, having help permit you to stay motivated and accountable.
- Celebrate Your Progress: Acknowledge and celebrate your achievements, regardless of how small they'll seem.
- Stay Positive: A fine mind-set can make a huge distinction for your motivation and outlook in your fitness adventure.
- Enjoy the Journey: Remember that health is a lifelong journey, so revel in the system and have fun every breakthrough.

Now, it's time to be able to begin your adventure with self belief. Believe in yourself, stay dedicated for your goals, and accept as true with the procedure. With dedication and perseverance, you may obtain the health and fitness effects you preference. So, take that first step today and embark at the direction to a healthier, happier you.

☀ HERE IS YOU FREE BONUS!
↳ SCAN HERE TO DOWNLOAD IT

4. All fitness levels welcome. Start at your level, push your boundaries.
5. Detailed guidance ensures injury-free, effective workouts.
6. Gym, home, full-body, the complete wellness package. Enhance your diet, boost wellness.

↳ SCAN HERE TO DOWNLOAD IT FOR FREE

Made in United States
Troutdale, OR
06/27/2024